interchange
FOURTH EDITION

Jack C. Richards

Series Editor: David Bohlke

CAMBRIDGE
UNIVERSITY PRESS

Intro
STUDENT'S BOOK

CAMBRIDGE
UNIVERSITY PRESS

University Printing House, Cambridge CB2 8BS, United Kingdom

One Liberty Plaza, 20th Floor, New York, NY 10006, USA

477 Williamstown Road, Port Melbourne, VIC 3207, Australia

4843/24, 2nd Floor, Ansari Road, Daryaganj, Delhi – 110002, India

79 Anson Road, #06–04/06, Singapore 079906

Cambridge University Press is part of the University of Cambridge.

It furthers the University's mission by disseminating knowledge in the pursuit of education, learning and research at the highest international levels of excellence.

www.cambridge.org
Information on this title: www.cambridge.org/9781107648661

First published 1994
Second edition 2000
Third edition 2005
40 39 38 37 36 35 34 33 32 31 30 29 28 27 26 25

Printed in Dubai by Oriental Press

A catalogue record for this publication is available from the British Library

ISBN 978-1-107-64866-1 Intro Student's Book with Self-study DVD
ISBN 978-1-107-68031-9 Intro Student's Book A with Self-study DVD
ISBN 978-1-107-61155-9 Intro Student's Book B with Self-study DVD
ISBN 978-1-107-64871-5 Intro Workbook
ISBN 978-1-107-67020-4 Intro Workbook A
ISBN 978-1-107-61537-3 Intro Workbook B
ISBN 978-1-107-64011-5 Intro Teacher's Edition with Assessment Audio CD/CD-ROM
ISBN 978-1-107-61034-7 Intro Class Audio CDs
ISBN 978-1-107-61495-6 Intro Full Contact with Self-study DVD-ROM
ISBN 978-1-107-68000-5 Intro Full Contact A with Self-study DVD-ROM
ISBN 978-1-107-69456-9 Intro Full Contact B with Self-study DVD-ROM

For a full list of components, visit www.cambridge.org/interchange

Cambridge University Press has no responsibility for the persistence or accuracy of URLs for external or third-party internet websites referred to in this publication, and does not guarantee that any content on such websites is, or will remain, accurate or appropriate. Information regarding prices, travel timetables, and other factual information given in this work is correct at the time of first printing but Cambridge University Press does not guarantee the accuracy of such information thereafter.

Art direction, book design, layout services, and photo research: Integra
Audio production: CityVox, NYC
Video production: Nesson Media Boston, Inc.

Welcome to *Interchange Fourth Edition*, the world's most successful English series!

Interchange offers a complete set of tools for learning how to communicate in English.

Student's Book
with NEW Self-study DVD-ROM

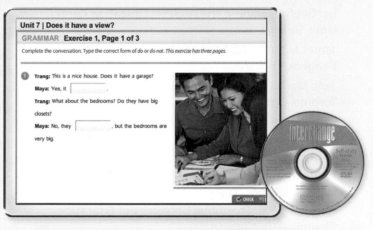

- **Complete video program** with additional **video exercises**

- Additional **vocabulary**, **grammar**, **speaking**, **listening**, and **reading** practice
- Printable **score reports** to submit to teachers

Available online

Interchange Arcade

- **Free** self-study website
- **Fun**, interactive, self-scoring activities
- Practice **vocabulary**, **grammar**, **listening**, and **reading**
- **MP3s** of the class audio program

Online Workbook

- A variety of **interactive activities** that correspond to each Student's Book lesson
- **Instant feedback** for hundreds of activities
- **Easy to use** with clear, easy-to-follow instructions
- Extra **listening practice**
- Simple tools for teachers to **monitor progress** such as scores, attendance, and time spent online

Author's acknowledgments

A great number of people contributed to the development of *Interchange Fourth Edition*. Particular thanks are owed to the reviewers using *Interchange, Third Edition* in the following schools and institutes – their insights and suggestions have helped define the content and format of the fourth edition:

Ian Geoffrey Hanley, **The Address Education Center**, Izmir, Turkey

James McBride, **AUA Language Center**, Bangkok, Thailand

Jane Merivale, **Centennial College**, Toronto, Ontario, Canada

Elva Elena Peña Andrade, **Centro de Auto Aprendizaje de Idiomas**, Nuevo León, Mexico

José Paredes, **Centro de Educación Continua de la Escuela Politécnica Nacional** (CEC-EPN), Quito, Ecuador

Chia-jung Tsai, **Changhua University of Education**, Changhua City, Taiwan

Kevin Liang, **Chinese Culture University**, Taipei, Taiwan

Roger Alberto Neira Perez, **Colegio Santo Tomás de Aquino**, Bogotá, Colombia

Teachers at **Escuela Miguel F. Martínez**, Monterrey, Mexico

Maria Virgínia Goulart Borges de Lebron, **Great Idiomas**, São Paulo, Brazil

Gina Kim, **Hoseo University**, Chungnam, South Korea

Heeyong Kim, Seoul, South Korea

Elisa Borges, **IBEU-Rio**, Rio de Janeiro, Brazil

Jason M. Ham, **Inha University**, Incheon, South Korea

Rita de Cássia S. Silva Miranda, **Instituto Batista de Idiomas**, Belo Horizonte, Brazil

Teachers at **Instituto Politécnico Nacional**, Mexico City, Mexico

Victoria M. Roberts and Regina Marie Williams, **Interactive College of Technology**, Chamblee, Georgia, USA

Teachers at **Internacional de Idiomas**, Mexico City, Mexico

Marcelo Serafim Godinho, **Life Idiomas**, São Paulo, Brazil

J. Kevin Varden, **Meiji Gakuin University**, Yokohama, Japan

Rosa Maria Valencia Rodríguez, Mexico City, Mexico

Chung-Ju Fan, **National Kinmen Institute of Technology**, Kinmen, Taiwan

Shawn Beasom, **Nihon Daigaku**, Tokyo, Japan

Gregory Hadley, **Niigata University of International and Information Studies**, Niigata, Japan

Chris Ruddenklau, **Osaka University of Economics and Law**, Osaka, Japan

Byron Roberts, **Our Lady of Providence Girls' High School**, Xindian City, Taiwan

Simon Banha, **Phil Young's English School**, Curitiba, Brazil

Flávia Gonçalves Carneiro Braathen, **Real English Center**, Viçosa, Brazil

Márcia Cristina Barboza de Miranda, **SENAC**, Recife, Brazil

Raymond Stone, **Seneca College of Applied Arts and Technology**, Toronto, Ontario, Canada

Gen Murai, **Takushoku University**, Tokyo, Japan

Teachers at **Tecnológico de Estudios Superiores de Ecatepec**, Mexico City, Mexico

Teachers at **Universidad Autónoma Metropolitana–Azcapotzalco**, Mexico City, Mexico

Teachers at **Universidad Autónoma de Nuevo León**, Monterrey, Mexico

Mary Grace Killian Reyes, **Universidad Autónoma de Tamaulipas**, Tampico Tamaulipas, Mexico

Teachers at **Universidad Estatal del Valle de Ecatepec**, Mexico City, Mexico

Teachers at **Universidad Nacional Autónoma de Mexico – Zaragoza**, Mexico City, Mexico

Teachers at **Universidad Nacional Autónoma de Mexico – Iztacala**, Mexico City, Mexico

Luz Edith Herrera Diaz, Veracruz, Mexico

Seri Park, **YBM PLS**, Seoul, South Korea

Self-assessment charts revised by Alex Tilbury
Grammar plus written by Karen Davy

Plan of Intro Book

Titles/Topics	Speaking	Grammar
UNIT 1 PAGES 2–7		
It's nice to meet you. Alphabet; greetings and leave-takings; names and titles of address; numbers 0–10, phone numbers, and email addresses	Introducing yourself and friends; saying hello and good-bye; asking for names and phone numbers	Possessive adjectives *my, your, his, her;* the verb *be;* affirmative statements and contractions
UNIT 2 PAGES 8–13		
What's this? Possessions, classroom objects, personal items, and locations in a room	Naming objects; asking for and giving the locations of objects	Articles *a, an,* and *the; this/these, it/they;* plurals; yes/no and *where* questions with *be;* prepositions of place: *in, in front of, behind, on, next to,* and *under*
PROGRESS CHECK PAGES 14–15		
UNIT 3 PAGES 16–21		
Where are you from? Cities and countries; adjectives of personality and appearance; numbers 11–103 and ages	Talking about cities and countries; asking for and giving information about place of origin, nationality, first language, and age; describing people	The verb *be:* affirmative and negative statements, yes/no questions, short answers, and Wh-questions
UNIT 4 PAGES 22–27		
Whose jeans are these? Clothing; colors; weather and seasons	Asking about and describing clothing and colors; talking about the weather and seasons; finding the owners of objects	Possessives: adjectives *our* and *their,* pronouns, names, and *whose;* present continuous statements and yes/no questions; conjunctions *and, but,* and *so;* placement of adjectives before nouns
PROGRESS CHECK PAGES 28–29		
UNIT 5 PAGES 30–35		
What are you doing? Clock time; times of the day; everyday activities	Asking for and telling time; asking about and describing current activities	Time expressions: *o'clock,* A.M., P.M., *noon, midnight, in the morning/ afternoon/evening, at 7:00/night/ midnight;* present continuous Wh-questions
UNIT 6 PAGES 36–41		
My sister works downtown. Transportation; family relationships; daily routines; days of the week	Asking for and giving information about how people go to work or school; talking about family members; describing daily and weekly routines	Simple present statements with regular and irregular verbs; simple present yes/no and Wh-questions; time expressions: *early, late, every day, on Sundays/weekends/ weekdays*
PROGRESS CHECK PAGES 42–43		
UNIT 7 PAGES 44–49		
Does it have a view? Houses and apartments; rooms; furniture	Asking about and describing houses and apartments; talking about the furniture in a room	Simple present short answers; *there is, there are; there's no, there isn't a, there are no, there aren't any*
UNIT 8 PAGES 50–55		
What do you do? Jobs and workplaces	Asking for and giving information about work; giving opinions about jobs; describing workday routines	Simple present Wh-questions with *do* and *does;* placement of adjectives after *be* and before nouns
PROGRESS CHECK PAGES 56–57		

Pronunciation/Listening	Writing/Reading	Interchange Activity
Linked sounds Listening for the spelling of names, phone numbers, and email addresses	Writing a list of names, phone numbers, and email addresses	"Famous classmates": Introducing yourself to new people **PAGE 114**
Plural -s endings Listening for the locations of objects	Writing the locations of objects	"Find the differences": Comparing two pictures of a room **PAGE 115**
Syllable stress Listening for countries, cities, and languages; listening to descriptions of people	Writing questions requesting personal information	"Board game": Finding out more about your classmates **PAGE 118**
The letters s and sh Listening for descriptions of clothing and colors	Writing questions about what people are wearing	"Celebrity fashions": Describing celebrities' clothing **PAGES 116–117**
Rising and falling intonation Listening for times of the day; listening to identify people's actions	Writing times of the day "Friends Across a Continent": Reading an online chat between two friends	"What's wrong with this picture?": Describing what's wrong with a picture **PAGE 119**
Third-person singular -s endings Listening for activities and days of the week	Writing about your weekly routine "What's Your Schedule Like?": Reading about three people's daily schedules	"Class survey": Finding out more about classmates' habits and routines **PAGE 120**
Words with th Listening to descriptions of homes; listening to people shop for furniture	Writing about your dream home "Unusual Homes": Reading about two unusual homes	"Find the differences": Comparing two apartments **PAGE 121**
Reduction of do Listening to people describe their jobs	Writing about jobs "Job Profiles": Reading about four unusual jobs	"The perfect job": Figuring out what job is right for you **PAGE 122**

Titles/Topics	Speaking	Grammar
UNIT 9 PAGES 58–63		
Do we need any eggs? Basic foods; breakfast foods; meals	Talking about food likes and dislikes; giving opinions about healthy and unhealthy foods; talking about foods you have and need; describing eating habits	Count and noncount nouns; *some* and *any*; adverbs of frequency: *always, usually, often, sometimes, hardly ever, never*
UNIT 10 PAGES 64–69		
What sports do you play? Sports; abilities and talents	Asking about free-time activities; asking for and giving information about abilities and talents	Simple present Wh-questions; *can* for ability; yes/no and Wh-questions with *can*
PROGRESS CHECK PAGES 70–71		
UNIT 11 PAGES 72–77		
What are you going to do? Months and dates; birthdays, holidays, festivals, and special days	Asking about birthdays; talking about plans for the evening, weekend, and other occasions	The future with *be going to*; yes/no and Wh-questions with *be going to*; future time expressions
UNIT 12 PAGES 78–83		
What's the matter? Parts of the body; health problems and advice; medications	Describing health problems; talking about common medications; giving advice for health problems	*Have* + noun; *feel* + adjective; negative and positive adjectives; imperatives
PROGRESS CHECK PAGES 84–85		
UNIT 13 PAGES 86–91		
You can't miss it. Stores and things you can buy there; tourist attractions	Talking about stores and other places; asking for and giving directions	Prepositions of place: *on, on the corner of, across from, next to, between*; giving directions with imperatives
UNIT 14 PAGES 92–97		
Did you have fun? Weekends; chores and fun activities; vacations; summer activities	Asking for and giving information about weekend and vacation activities	Simple past statements with regular and irregular verbs; simple past yes/no questions and short answers
PROGRESS CHECK PAGES 98–99		
UNIT 15 PAGES 100–105		
Where did you grow up? Biographical information; years; school days	Asking for and giving information about date and place of birth; describing school experiences and memories	Statements and questions with the past of *be*; Wh-questions with *did, was,* and *were*
UNIT 16 PAGES 106–111		
Can she call you later? Locations; telephone calls; invitations; going out with friends	Describing people's locations; making, accepting, and declining invitations; making excuses	Prepositional phrases; subject and object pronouns; invitations with *Do you want to…?* and *Would you like to…?*; verb + *to*
PROGRESS CHECK PAGES 112–113		
GRAMMAR PLUS PAGES 132–151		

Pronunciation/Listening	Writing/Reading	Interchange Activity
Sentence stress Listening for people's food preferences	Writing about mealtime habits "Eating for Good Luck": Reading about foods people eat for good luck in the new year	"Snack survey": Taking a survey about snacks you eat and comparing answers PAGE 123
Pronunciation of *can* and *can't* Listening for people's favorite sports to watch or play; listening to people talk about their abilities	Writing questions about sports "An Interview with Shawn Johnson": Reading about the life of an Olympic athlete	"Hidden talents": Finding out more about your classmates' hidden talents PAGE 124
Reduction of *going to* Listening to people talk about their evening plans	Writing about weekend plans "What Are You Going to Do on Your Birthday?": Reading about birthday customs in different places	"Guessing game": Making guesses about a classmate's plans PAGE 125
Sentence intonation Listening to people talk about health problems; listening for medications	Writing advice for health problems "10 Simple Ways to Improve Your Health": Reading about ways to improve your health	"Helpful advice": Giving advice for some common problems PAGE 126
Compound nouns Listening to people talk about shopping; listening to directions	Writing directions "Edinburgh's Royal Mile": Reading about popular tourist attractions in Edinburgh, Scotland	"Giving directions": Asking for directions in a neighborhood PAGES 127, 128
Simple past *-ed* endings Listening to people talk about their past summer activities	Writing about last weekend "Did You Have a Good Weekend?": Reading about four people's weekend experiences	"Past and present": Comparing your classmates' present lives with their childhoods PAGE 129
Negative contractions Listening for places and dates of birth	Writing questions about a young person's life "Turning Pain to Gain": Reading about a young woman's life	"Life events": Making a time line of important events in your life PAGE 130
Reduction of *want to* and *have to* Listening to phone conversations; listening to voice-mail messages	Writing about weekend plans "Around Los Angeles: This Weekend": Reading about events on a web page	"Let's make a date!": Making plans with your classmates PAGE 131

1 It's nice to meet you.

1 CONVERSATION *My name is Jennifer Miller.*

A ▶ Listen and practice.

Michael: Hello. My name is Michael Ota.
Jennifer: Hi. My name is Jennifer Miller.
Michael: It's nice to meet you, Jennifer.
Jennifer: Nice to meet you, too.
Michael: I'm sorry. What's your last name again?
Jennifer: It's Miller.

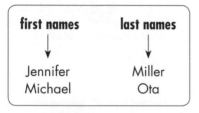

first names	last names
↓	↓
Jennifer	Miller
Michael	Ota

B **PAIR WORK** Introduce yourself to your partner.

2 SNAPSHOT

▶ Listen and practice.

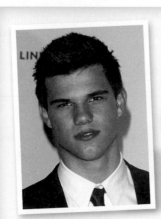

Popular Names in the U.S.
for Both Males and Females

Taylor Jordan Casey Jamie Riley
Jessie Hayden Peyton Quinn Rory

Taylor Lautner

Taylor Swift

Source: www.babynames1000.com

Circle the names you know.
What are some popular names for males in your country? for females?
What names are popular for both males and females?

2

3 GRAMMAR FOCUS

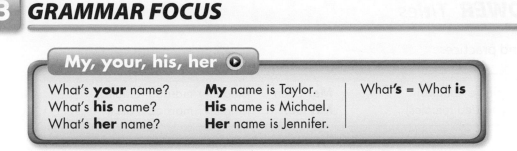

My, your, his, her ▶

What's **your** name?	**My** name is Taylor.	What**'s** = What **is**
What's **his** name?	**His** name is Michael.	
What's **her** name?	**Her** name is Jennifer.	

A Complete the conversations. Use *my*, *your*, *his*, or *her*.

1. A: Hello. What's ....._your_..... name?
   B: Hi. .... name is Antonio.
      What's .... name?
   A: .... name is Nicole.

2. A: What's .... name?
   B: .... name is Michael.
   A: And what's .... name?
   B: .... name is Jennifer.

B **PAIR WORK** Practice the conversations with a partner.

4 SPELLING NAMES

A ▶ Listen and practice.

A B C D E F G H I J K L M N O P Q R S T U V W X Y Z
a b c d e f g h i j k l m n o p q r s t u v w x y z

B ▶ **CLASS ACTIVITY** Listen and practice. Then practice with your own names. Make a list of your classmates' names.

A: What's your name?
B: My name is Sarah Conner.
A: Is that S-A-R-A-H?
B: Yes, that's right.
A: How do you spell your last name? C-O-N-N-O-R?
B: No, it's C-O-N-N-E-R.

> <u>My Classmates</u>
> Sarah Conner
> Jennifer Miller

5 LISTENING *First names*

▶ How do you spell the names? Listen and check (✓) the correct answers.

1. ☐ Kara   2. ☐ Mark   3. ☐ Shawn   4. ☐ Sophia
   ☐ Cara   ☐ Marc   ☐ Sean   ☐ Sofia

6 WORD POWER Titles

A ▶ Listen and practice.

Miss Ito	(single females)	**Ms.** Chen	(single or married females)
Mrs. Morgan	(married females)	**Mr.** Garcia	(single or married males)

B ▶ Listen and write the titles.

1. .... Lopez   2. .... Smith   3. .... Kim   4. .... Anderson

7 SAYING HELLO

A ▶ Listen and practice.

B CLASS ACTIVITY Go around the class. Greet your classmates formally (with titles) and informally (without titles).

8 CONVERSATION *He's over there.*

A ▶ Listen and practice.

Jennifer: Excuse me. Are you
Steven Carson?
David: No, I'm not. He's over there.
Jennifer: Oh, I'm sorry.

Jennifer: Steven? This is your book.
Steven: Oh, thank you. You're in my
class, right?
Jennifer: Yes, I am. I'm Jennifer Miller.

Steven: Hey, David, this is Jennifer.
She's in our math class.
David: Hi, Jennifer.
Jennifer: Hi, David. Nice to meet you.

B GROUP WORK Greet a classmate. Then introduce him or her to
another classmate.

"Hey, Ming, this is . . ."

9 GRAMMAR FOCUS

> ### The verb be ▶
>
> | | |
> |---|---|
> | **I'm** Jennifer Miller. | **Are you** Steven Carson? |
> | **You're** in my class. | Yes, **I am**. |
> | **She's** in our class. (**Jennifer is** in our class.) | No, **I'm not**. |
> | **He's** over there. (**Steven is** over there.) | |
> | **It's** Miller. (**My last name is** Miller.) | How **are you**? |
> | | **I'm** fine. |
>
> **I'm** = I am
> **You're** = You are
> **He's** = He is
> **She's** = She is
> **It's** = It is

A Complete the conversation with the correct words in parentheses.
Then practice with a partner.

David: Hello, Jennifer. How ......*are*........ (is / are) you?
Jennifer: .... (She's / I'm) fine, thanks.
.... (I'm / It's) sorry – what's your name again?
David: .... (He's / It's) David – David Medina.
Jennifer: That's right! David, this .... (is / am) Sarah Conner.
.... (She's / He's) in our math class.
David: Hi, Sarah. .... (I'm / It's) nice to meet you.
Sarah: Hi, David. I think .... (you're / I'm) in my English class, too.
David: Oh, right! Yes, I .... (are / am).

B Complete the conversations. Then practice in groups.

Nicole: Excuse me. ....Are....... you Steven Carson?
David: No, ... not. My name ....
David Medina. Steven .... over there.
Nicole: Oh, sorry.

Nicole: .... you Steven Carson?
Steven: Yes, I ....
Nicole: Hi. .... Nicole Johnson.
Steven: Oh, ... in my math class, right?
Nicole: Yes, I ....
Steven: .... nice to meet you.

C CLASS ACTIVITY Write your name on a
piece of paper. Put the papers in a bag. Then
take a different paper. Find the other student.

A: Excuse me. Are you Jin-sook Cho?
B: No, I'm not. She's over there.
A: Hi. Are you Jin-sook Cho?
C: Yes, I am.

10 PRONUNCIATION *Linked sounds*

▶ Listen and practice. Notice the linked sounds.

I'm Antonio.   She's over there.   You're in my class.

11 PERSONAL INFORMATION

A ▶ Listen and practice.

0	1	2	3	4	5	6	7	8	9	10
zero (oh)	one	two	three	four	five	six	seven	eight	nine	ten

B ▶ PAIR WORK Practice these phone numbers and
email addresses. Then listen and check your answers.

Allison Parker
402-555-2301 (work phone)
646-486-1004 (cell phone)
aparker1@cup.org (email address)

at   dot

KENJI MORI
212-924-1764 (home phone)
643-555-2285 (cell phone)
kenjimori09@cambridge.org (email address)

"Her name is Allison Parker. Her work phone number is
four-oh-two, five-five-five, two-three-oh-one. Her cell . . ."

12 LISTENING *A class list*

A ▶ Jennifer and Michael are making a list of classmates' phone numbers and email addresses. Listen and complete the list.

Name	☎ Phone number	@ Email address
David Medina	212-555-1937	
Sarah Conner		
Steven Carson		
Nicole Johnson		

B **CLASS ACTIVITY** Make a list of your classmates' names, phone numbers, and email addresses.

A: What's your name?
B: I'm Anna Silva.

A: And what's your phone number?
B: It's 201-555-2491.

13 INTERCHANGE 1 *Famous classmates*

Meet some "famous classmates." Go to Interchange 1 on page 114.

14 SAYING GOOD-BYE

A ▶ Listen and practice.

1. See you later, Matthew.
   Bye-bye, Lisa.

2. See you tomorrow, Alex.
   Bye, Mr. Garcia.

3. Good-bye. Have a great weekend.
   Thank you. You, too.

4. Good-bye, Miss Chen. Have a good evening!
   Good night, Mrs. Morgan.

B **CLASS ACTIVITY** Go around the room. Say good-bye to your classmates and teacher.

2 What's this?

▶ Listen and practice.

What's in your bag?

☐ a hairbrush

☐ an umbrella

☐ sunglasses

☐ keys

☐ a laptop

☐ a cell phone

☐ a wallet

☐ a camera

Source: Based on interviews with people between the ages of 16 and 30

Check (✓) the things in your bag.
What other things are in your bag?

2 ARTICLES *Classroom objects*

A ▶ Listen. Complete these sentences with *a* or *an*.

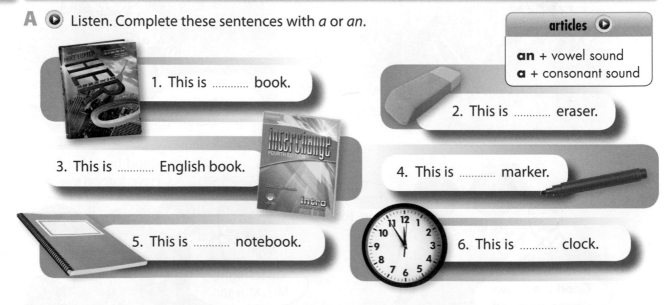

articles ▶
an + vowel sound
a + consonant sound

1. This is .... book.

2. This is .... eraser.

3. This is .... English book.

4. This is .... marker.

5. This is .... notebook.

6. This is .... clock.

B **PAIR WORK** Find and spell these things in your classroom.

board	desk	eraser	pen	wall
book bag	dictionary	map	pencil	wastebasket
chair	door	notebook	table	window

A: This is a board.
B: How do you spell *board*?
A: B-O-A-R-D.

CONVERSATION *It's . . . interesting.*

▶ Listen and practice.

Wendy: Wow! What are these?
Helen: They're earrings.
Wendy: Oh, cool! Thank you, Helen.
    They're great!
Helen: You're welcome.
  Rex: Now open this box!
Wendy: OK. Uh, what's this?
  Rex: It's a scarf.
Wendy: Oh. It's . . . interesting.
    Thank you, Rex. It's very nice.

4 **PRONUNCIATION** *Plural -s endings*

A ▶ Listen and practice. Notice the pronunciation of the plural **-s** endings.

s = /z/		s = /s/		(e)s = /ɪz/	
earring	earring**s**	desk	desk**s**	pencil case	pencil case**s**
phone	phone**s**	laptop	laptop**s**	class	class**es**
book bag	book bag**s**	wastebasket	wastebasket**s**	box	box**es**

B Say the plural forms of these nouns. Then complete the chart.

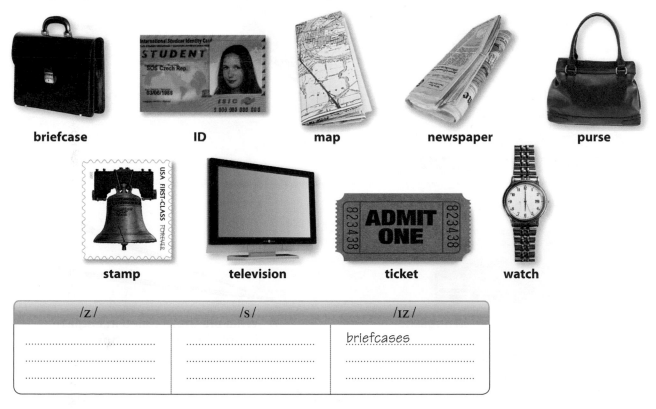

briefcase   **ID**   **map**   **newspaper**   **purse**

stamp   **television**   **ticket**   **watch**

/z/	/s/	/ɪz/
		briefcases

C ▶ Listen and check your answers.

GRAMMAR FOCUS

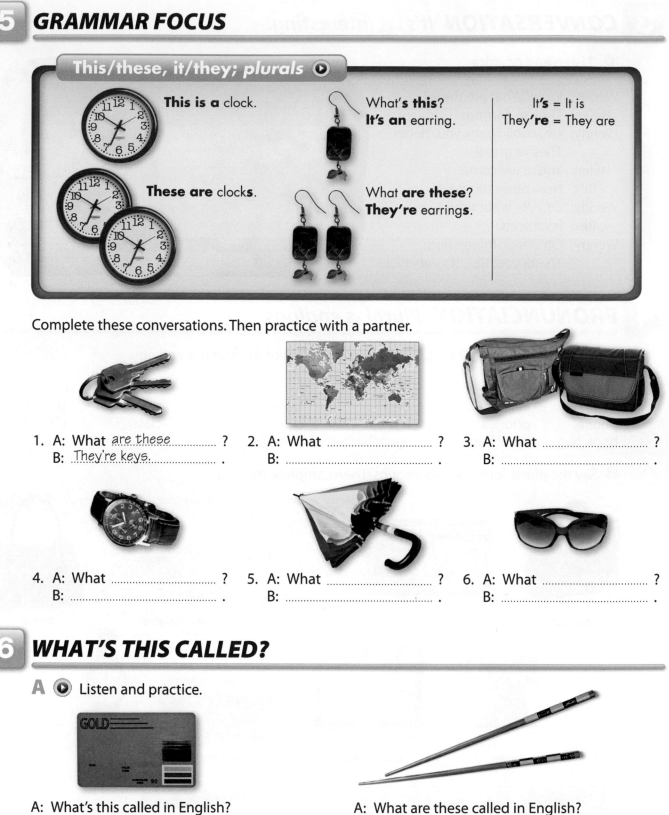

This/these, it/they; *plurals*

This is a clock.

These are clocks.

What's **this**?
It's an earring.

What **are these**?
They're earrings.

It's = It is
They're = They are

Complete these conversations. Then practice with a partner.

1. A: What are these ?
   B: They're keys. .

2. A: What ?
   B: .

3. A: What ?
   B: .

4. A: What ?
   B: .

5. A: What ?
   B: .

6. A: What ?
   B: .

6 WHAT'S THIS CALLED?

A Listen and practice.

GOLD

A: What's this called in English?
B: I don't know.
C: It's a credit card.
A: How do you spell that?
C: C-R-E-D-I-T C-A-R-D.

A: What are these called in English?
B: I think they're called chopsticks.
A: How do you spell that?
B: C-H-O-P-S-T-I-C-K-S.

B GROUP WORK Choose four things. Put them on a desk.
Then ask about the name and spelling of each thing.

7 CONVERSATION *Oh, no!*

▶ Listen and practice.

Kate: Oh, no! Where are my car keys?
Joe: I don't know. Are they in your purse?
Kate: No, they're not.
Joe: Maybe they're on the table in the restaurant.

Server: Excuse me. Are these your keys?
Kate: Yes, they are. Thank you!
Server: You're welcome. And is this your wallet?
Kate: Hmm. No, it's not. Where's your wallet, Joe?
Joe: It's in my pocket. . . . Wait a minute! That *is* my wallet!

8 GRAMMAR FOCUS

> ### Yes/No and where questions with be ▶
>
> **Is this** your wallet?
>   Yes, **it is**. / No, **it's not**.
>
> **Are these** your keys?
>   Yes, **they are**. / No, **they're not**.
>
> **Where's** your wallet?
>   **It's** in my pocket.
>
> **Where are** my keys?
>   **They're** on the table.

A Complete these conversations. Then practice with a partner.

1. A: ....Is.... this your umbrella?
   B: No, ... not.
   A: .... these your keys?
   B: Yes, ... are. Thanks!

2. A: Where .... my glasses?
   B: Are .... your glasses?
   A: No, they're ....
   B: Wait! .... they in your pocket?
   A: Yes, ... are. Thanks!

3. A: Where .... your sunglasses?
   B: .... on the table.
   A: No, ... not. They're *my* sunglasses!
   B: You're right. My sunglasses .... in my purse.

4. A: .... this my pen?
   B: No, ... not. It's *my* pen.
   A: Sorry. .... is my pen?
   B: .... on your desk.
   A: Oh, you're right!

B **GROUP WORK** Put three of your things in a bag. Then choose three different things. Find the owner of each thing.

A: Is this your pen, Yuko?
B: No, it's not.

A: Are these your keys, Sergio?
C: Let me see. Yes, they are.

9 WORD POWER *Prepositions; article* the

A ▶ Listen and practice.

Where are **the** keys?
The keys are in **the** box.

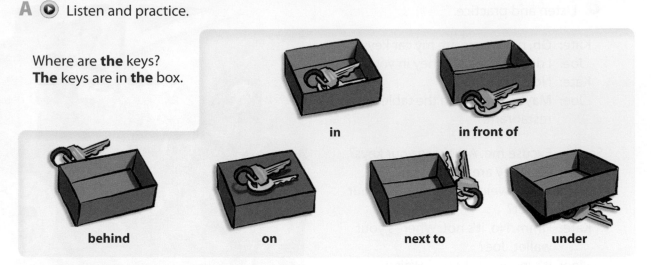

in in front of

behind on next to under

B ▶ Complete these sentences. Then listen and check your answers.

1. The books are *in the book bag* .

2. The cell phone is ....

3. The map is ....

4. The chair is ....

5. The wallet is ....

6. The sunglasses are ....

C PAIR WORK Ask and answer questions about the pictures in part B.

A: Where are the books?
B: They're in the book bag.

10 LISTENING *Kate's things*

▶ Listen. Where are Kate's things? Match the things with their locations.

1. earrings ...*d*...
2. watch ....
3. sunglasses ....
4. camera ....

a. under the table
b. in front of the television
c. on the chair
d. in her purse

11 WHERE ARE JOE'S THINGS?

PAIR WORK Now help Joe find his things. Ask and answer questions.

briefcase	cell phone	newspaper	umbrella
camera	glasses	notebook	wallet

A: Where's his briefcase?
B: It's on the table.

12 INTERCHANGE 2 *Find the differences*

Compare two pictures of a room. Go to Interchange 2 on page 115.

Units 1–2 Progress check

SELF-ASSESSMENT

How well can you do these things? Check (✓) the boxes.

I can	Very well	OK	A little
Introduce myself and other people (Ex. 1)	☐	☐	☐
Say hello and good-bye (Ex. 1)	☐	☐	☐
Exchange contact information, e.g., phone numbers (Ex. 2)	☐	☐	☐
Understand names for everyday objects and possessions (Ex. 3)	☐	☐	☐
Ask and answer questions about where things are (Ex. 4, 5)	☐	☐	☐

1 HOW ARE YOU?

A Complete the conversation. Use the sentences and questions in the box.

Matt: Hi. How are you?
Nicki: I'm fine, thanks. ....
Matt: Pretty good, thanks. ....
Nicki: And I'm Nicki White.
Matt: ....
Nicki: Nice to meet you, too. ....
Matt: Yes, I am.
Nicki: ....
Matt: See you in class.

> My name is Matt Carlson.
> Oh, are you in my English class?
> How about you?
> ✓ Hi. How are you?
> It's nice to meet you, Nicki.
> Well, have a good day.

B **PAIR WORK** Practice the conversation from part A. Use your own information. Then introduce your partner to a classmate.

"Malena, this is my friend. His name is Tetsu. . . ."

2 IS YOUR PHONE NUMBER . . . ?

CLASS ACTIVITY Write your phone number on a piece of paper. Then put the papers in a bag. Take a different paper and find the owner. Write his or her name on the paper.

A: Ali, is your phone number 781-555-1532?
B: No, it's not. Sorry!
A: Mila, is your . . . ?

3 *LISTENING* *What's this? What are these?*

Listen to the conversations. Number the pictures from 1 to 6.

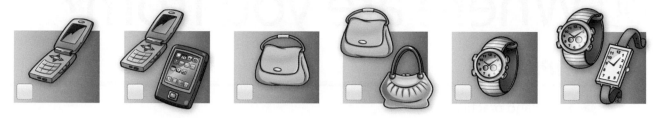

4 WHAT'S WRONG WITH THIS ROOM?

A What's wrong with this room? Make a list. Find 10 things.

The chair is on the desk.

B **PAIR WORK** Ask and answer *Where* questions about the picture.

A: Where's the chair?
B: It's on the desk.

5 YES OR NO GAME

Write five yes/no questions about the picture in Exercise 4. Three have "yes" answers, and two have "no" answers. Then ask a partner the questions.

A: Is the chair behind the clock?
B: No, it isn't.

WHAT'S NEXT?

Look at your Self-assessment again. Do you need to review anything?

3 Where are you from?

SNAPSHOT

▶ Listen and practice.

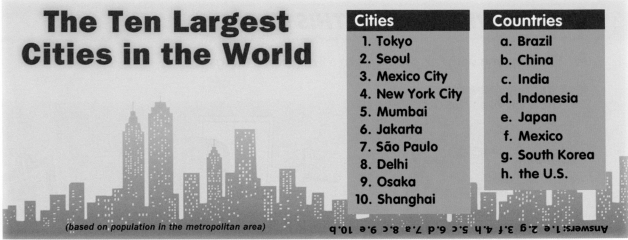

The Ten Largest Cities in the World

Cities	Countries
1. Tokyo	a. Brazil
2. Seoul	b. China
3. Mexico City	c. India
4. New York City	d. Indonesia
5. Mumbai	e. Japan
6. Jakarta	f. Mexico
7. São Paulo	g. South Korea
8. Delhi	h. the U.S.
9. Osaka	
10. Shanghai	

(based on population in the metropolitan area)

Answers: 1. e 2. g 3. f 4. h 5. c 6. d 7. a 8. c 9. e 10. b

Source: www.worldatlas.com

Match the cities with the countries. Then check your answers at the bottom of the Snapshot. What other large cities are in each country? What large cities are in your country?

CONVERSATION *Are you from Seoul?*

A ▶ Listen and practice.

Tim: Are you from California, Jessica?
Jessica: Well, my family is in California now, but we're from South Korea originally.
Tim: Oh, my mother is Korean – from Seoul! Are you from Seoul?
Jessica: No, we're not. We're from Daejeon.
Tim: So is your first language Korean?
Jessica: Yes, it is.

B ▶ Listen to Jessica and Tim talk to Tony, Natasha, and Monique. Check (✓) True or False.

WELCOME NEW STUDENTS

	True	False
1. Tony is from Italy.	☐	☐
2. Natasha is from New York.	☐	☐
3. Monique's first language is English.	☐	☐

16

GRAMMAR FOCUS

Negative statements and yes/no questions with be

I'm not from New York.	**Are you** from California?		**I am.**	**I'm**	**not.**
You're not late.	**Am I** early?		**you are.**	**you're**	**not.**
She's not from Russia.	**Is she** from Brazil?		**she is.**	**she's**	**not.**
He's not from Italy.	**Is he** from Chile?	Yes, **he is.**	No,	**he's**	**not.**
It's not English.	**Is it** Korean?		**it is.**	**it's**	**not.**
We're not from Japan.	**Are you** from China?		**we are.**	**we're**	**not.**
You're not early.	**Are we** late?		**you are.**	**you're**	**not.**
They're not in Mexico.	**Are they** in Canada?		**they are.**	**they're**	**not.**

We**'re** = We are

A Complete the conversations. Then practice with a partner.

Kyoto, Japan

1. A: Hiroshi, ...*are*........ you and Maiko from Japan?
   B: Yes, we ....
   A: Oh? .... you from Tokyo?
   B: No, ... not. .... from Kyoto.

2. A: .... Laura from the U.S.?
   B: No, ... not. She's from the U.K.
   A: .... she from London?
   B: Yes, she .... But her parents are from Italy. .... not from the U.K. originally.
   A: .... Laura's first language Italian?
   B: No, ... not. .... English.

3. A: .... Selina and Carlos from Mexico?
   B: No, ... not. .... from Brazil.
   A: .... you from Brazil, too?
   B: No, ... not. I'm from Peru.
   A: So, ... your first language Spanish?
   B: Yes, it ....

Lima, Peru

B Match the questions with the answers. Then practice with a partner.

1. Are you and your family from Canada? ....*d*....
2. Is your first language English? ....
3. Are you Japanese? ....
4. Is Mr. Ho from Hong Kong? ....
5. Is your mother from the U.S.? ....

a. No, he's not. He's from Singapore.
b. Yes, she is. She's from California.
c. No, it's not. It's Japanese.
d. No, we're not. We're from Australia.
e. Yes, we are. We're from Kyoto.

C **PAIR WORK** Write five questions like the ones in part B. Then ask and answer your questions with a partner.

4 PRONUNCIATION *Syllable stress*

A Listen and practice. Notice the syllable stress.

● ●	● ●	● ● ●	● ● ●
China	Japan	Canada	Morocco
Turkey	Brazil	Mexico	Malaysia
....	....	....	....
....	....	....	....

B ▶ What is the syllable stress in these words? Add the words to the chart in part A. Then listen and check.

English	Spanish	Arabic	Korean
Mexican	Honduras	Chinese	Peru

C GROUP WORK Are the words in part A countries, nationalities, or languages? Make a chart and add more words.

Countries	Nationalities	Languages
China	Chinese	Chinese
Mexico	Mexican	Spanish

5 WHERE ARE THEY FROM?

A Where are these people from? Check (✓) your guesses.

Penelope Cruz
☐ Mexico
☐ France
☐ Spain

Robert Pattinson
☐ the U.S.
☐ the U.K.
☐ Canada

Haru Nomura
☐ South Korea
☐ Japan
☐ China

Cate Blanchett
☐ Australia
☐ New Zealand
☐ South Africa

Javier Hernández
☐ Brazil
☐ Mexico
☐ Chile

B PAIR WORK Compare your guesses. Then check your answers at the bottom of the page.

A: Is Penelope Cruz from Mexico?
B: No, she's not.
A: Is she from France?

Answers: 1. Spain 2. the U.K. 3. Japan 4. Australia 5. Mexico

6 CONVERSATION *He's cute.*

▶ Listen and practice.

Emma: Who's that?
Jill: He's my brother.
Emma: Wow! He's cute. What's his name?
Jill: James. We call him Jim.
Emma: Oh, how old is he?
Jill: He's twenty-one years old.
Emma: What's he like? Is he nice?
Jill: Yes, he is – and he's very smart, too!
Emma: And who's that?
Jill: My sister Tammy. She's only twelve.
She's the baby of the family.

7 NUMBERS AND AGES

A ▶ Listen and practice.

11 eleven	**21** twenty-one	**40** forty
12 twelve	**22** twenty-two	**50** fifty
13 thirteen	**23** twenty-three	**60** sixty
14 fourteen	**24** twenty-four	**70** seventy
15 fifteen	**25** twenty-five	**80** eighty
16 sixteen	**26** twenty-six	**90** ninety
17 seventeen	**27** twenty-seven	**100** one hundred
18 eighteen	**28** twenty-eight	**101** one hundred (and) one
19 nineteen	**29** twenty-nine	**102** one hundred (and) two
20 twenty	**30** thirty	**103** one hundred (and) three

B ▶ Listen and practice. Notice the word stress.

thirteen – thirty   fourteen – forty   fifteen – fifty   sixteen – sixty

C **PAIR WORK** Look at the people in Jill's family for one minute.
Then close your books. How old are they? Tell your partner.

A. Helen – 76   **B.** Howard – 52   **C.** Jackie – 49   **D.** Megan – 23   **E.** Tim and Tom – 14

Wh-questions with be ▶

What's your name?
My name is Jill.
Where are you from?
I'm from Canada.
How are you today?
I'm just fine.

Who's that?
He's my brother.
How old is he?
He's twenty-one.
What's he like?
He's very nice.

Who are they?
They're my classmates.
Where are they from?
They're from Rio.
What's Rio like?
It's very beautiful.

Who**'s** = Who is

A Complete the conversations with Wh-questions.
Then practice with a partner.

1. A: Look! Who's that .... ?
   B: Oh, he's a new student.
   A: .... ?
   B: I think his name is Ming.
   A: Ming? .... ?
   B: He's from China.

2. A: Serhat, ... ?
   B: I'm from Turkey – from Istanbul.
   A: .... ?
   B: Istanbul is very old and beautiful.
   A: .... ?
   B: My last name is Erdogan.

3. A: Hi, John. .... ?
   B: I'm just fine. My friend Teresa is here
      this week – from Argentina.
   A: Oh, cool. .... ?
   B: She's really friendly.
   A: .... ?
   B: She's twenty-eight years old.

B **PAIR WORK** Write five Wh-questions about your partner and five Wh-questions
about your partner's best friend. Then ask and answer the questions.

Partner	Partner's best friend
Where are you from?	Who's your best friend?

9 WORD POWER Descriptions

A ▶ Listen and practice.

a. pretty	d. talkative	g. serious	j. tall	m. thin
b. handsome	e. quiet	h. shy	k. friendly	
c. good-looking	f. funny	i. short	l. heavy	

B PAIR WORK Complete the chart with words from part A. Add two more words to each list. Then describe your personality and appearance to a partner.

Personality			Appearance		
talkative	....	....	pretty	....	....
....	....	....	....	....	....
....	....	....	....	....	....

"I'm funny, smart, and very handsome."

10 LISTENING Who's that?

▶ Listen to three descriptions. Check (✓) the two correct words for each description.

1. Elena is . . .   ☐ short   ☐ pretty   ☐ friendly
2. Marco is . . .   ☐ tall   ☐ nice   ☐ shy
3. Andrew is . . .   ☐ talkative   ☐ funny   ☐ friendly

11 INTERCHANGE 3 Board game

Play a board game with your classmates. Go to Interchange 3 on page 118.

4 Whose jeans are these?

1 WORD POWER Clothes

A ▶ Listen and practice.

CLOTHES FOR WORK

tie
shirt
scarf
blouse
belt
skirt
jacket
pants } suit
coat
shoes
high heels

raincoat
dress

CLOTHES FOR LEISURE

hat
cap
sweater
T-shirt
shorts
gloves
jeans
socks
boots
sneakers

pajamas
swimsuits

B Complete the chart with words from part A.

Clothes for warm weather	Clothes for cold weather
....	....
....	....
....	....
....	....

C **PAIR WORK** Look around the classroom. What clothes do you see? Tell a partner.

"I see jeans, a sweater, boots, and . . ."

2 COLORS

A ▶ Listen and practice.

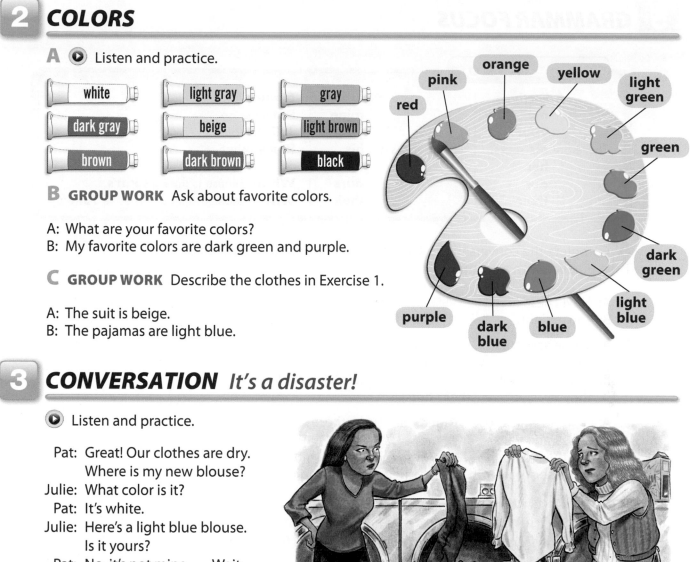

white | light gray | gray
dark gray | beige | light brown
brown | dark brown | black

red · pink · orange · yellow · light green · green · dark green · light blue · blue · dark blue · purple

B **GROUP WORK** Ask about favorite colors.

A: What are your favorite colors?
B: My favorite colors are dark green and purple.

C **GROUP WORK** Describe the clothes in Exercise 1.

A: The suit is beige.
B: The pajamas are light blue.

3 CONVERSATION *It's a disaster!*

▶ Listen and practice.

Pat: Great! Our clothes are dry. Where is my new blouse?
Julie: What color is it?
Pat: It's white.
Julie: Here's a light blue blouse. Is it yours?
Pat: No, it's not mine. . . . Wait. It *is* mine. It's a disaster!
Julie: Oh, no! *All* our clothes are light blue.
Pat: Here's the problem. It's these new blue jeans. Whose jeans are these?
Julie: Uh, they're mine. Sorry.

4 PRONUNCIATION *The letters s and sh*

A ▶ Listen and practice. Notice the pronunciation of **s** and **sh**.

1. **s**uit   **s**ocks   **s**carf
2. **sh**irt   **sh**orts   **sh**oes

B Read the sentences. Pay attention to the pronunciation of **s** and **sh**.

1. This is **S**andra's new **sh**irt.
2. These are **S**am's purple **sh**oes!
3. Where are my **sh**oes and **s**ocks?
4. My **sh**orts and T-**sh**irts are blue!

Possessives ⊙

Adjectives	Pronouns	Names	
my	**mine**	**Pat's** blouse	/s/
your	**yours**	**Julie's** jeans	/z/
These are **his** socks.	These socks are **his**.	**Rex's** T-shirt	/ɪz/
her	**hers**		
our	**ours**	**Whose** blouse is this? It's **Pat's**.	
their	**theirs**	**Whose** jeans are these? They're **Julie's**.	

A Complete the conversations with the correct words in parentheses. Then practice with a partner.

1. A: Hey! These aren't ......*our*........ (our / ours) clothes!
   B: You're right. .... (Our / Ours) are over there.

2. A: These aren't .... (my / mine) gloves. Are they .... (your / yours)?
   B: No, they're not .... (my / mine). Ask Sally. Maybe they're .... (her / hers).

3. A: .... (Whose / Yours) T-shirts are these? Are they Julie's and Pat's?
   B: No, they're not .... (their / theirs) T-shirts. But these socks are .... (their / theirs). And these shorts are .... (your / yours).

B **CLASS ACTIVITY** Put one of your things in a box. Then choose a different thing from the box. Go around the class and find the owner.

A: Diego, is this watch yours?
B: No, it's not mine. Maybe it's Rex's.

6 **LISTENING** *His shirt is green.*

A ⊙ Listen to someone describe these clothes. Number the pictures from 1 to 6.

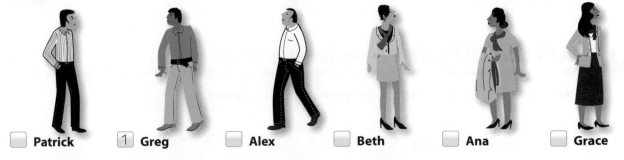

☐ **Patrick**   ☐ **1** **Greg**   ☐ **Alex**   ☐ **Beth**   ☐ **Ana**   ☐ **Grace**

B **PAIR WORK** Now talk about the people. What colors are their clothes?

A: What color is Patrick's shirt?
B: It's green and white.

7 SNAPSHOT

Listen and practice.

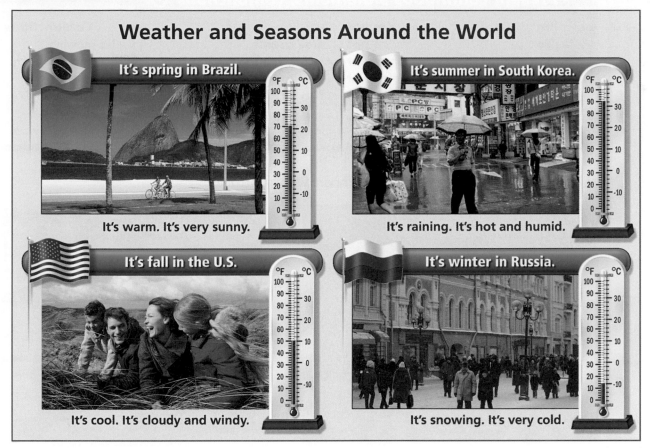

Weather and Seasons Around the World

It's spring in Brazil.
It's warm. It's very sunny.

It's summer in South Korea.
It's raining. It's hot and humid.

It's fall in the U.S.
It's cool. It's cloudy and windy.

It's winter in Russia.
It's snowing. It's very cold.

Source: *Yahoo! Travel*

What season is it now?
What's the weather like today?
What's your favorite season?

8 CONVERSATION *It's really cold!*

Listen and practice.

Pat: Oh, no!
Julie: What's the matter?
Pat: It's snowing! And it's windy, so it's really cold.
Julie: Are you wearing your gloves?
Pat: No, I'm not. They're at home.
Julie: What about your scarf?
Pat: It's at home, too.
Julie: Well, you're wearing your coat.
Pat: But my coat isn't very warm. And I'm not wearing boots!
Julie: Let's take a taxi.
Pat: Good idea!

Whose jeans are these? ▪ **25**

Present continuous statements; conjunctions ▶

		OR:		**Conjunctions**
I**'m**	I**'m not**			It's snowing,
You**'re**	You**'re not**	You **aren't**		**and** it's windy.
She**'s wearing** shoes.	She**'s not**	She **isn't wearing** boots.		It's sunny,
We**'re**	We**'re not**	We **aren't**		**but** it's cold.
They**'re**	They**'re not**	They **aren't**		It's windy,
It**'s snowing**.	It**'s not**	It **isn't raining**.		**so** it's very cold.

A Complete these sentences. Then compare with a partner.

My name is Claire. I ˙m wearing a green suit today. I .... high heels, too. It's raining, but I .... a raincoat.

It's very hot today. Toshi and Noriko .... shorts and T-shirts. It's really sunny, so they .... sunglasses.

Phil .... a suit today – he .... pants and a jacket. He .... a light blue shirt, but he .... a tie.

It's cold today, but Kathy .... a coat. She .... gloves and a hat. She .... boots. She .... sneakers.

Are you **wearing** gloves?	Yes, I **am**.	No, I**'m not**.
Is she **wearing** boots?	Yes, she **is**.	No, she**'s not**./No, she **isn't**.
Are they **wearing** sunglasses?	Yes, they **are**.	No, they**'re not**./No, they **aren't**.

B **PAIR WORK** Ask and answer these questions about the people in part A.

1. Is Claire wearing a green suit?
2. Is she wearing a raincoat?
3. Is she wearing high heels?
4. Are Toshi and Noriko wearing swimsuits?
5. Are they wearing jackets?
6. Are they wearing sunglasses?

7. Is Phil wearing brown pants?
8. Is he wearing a blue shirt?
9. Is he wearing a tie?
10. Is Kathy wearing boots?
11. Is she wearing a coat?
12. Is she wearing a hat and gloves?

A: Is Claire wearing a green suit?
B: Yes, she is. Is she wearing a raincoat?
A: No, she's not. OR No, she isn't.

adjective + noun

My suit is black.
I'm wearing a **black suit**.

C Write four more questions about the people in part A. Then ask a partner the questions.

10 LISTENING *He's wearing a T-shirt!*

A ▶ Listen. Write the names **Bruce, Beth, Jon, Anita,** and **Nick** in the correct boxes.

| | | | | Bruce |

B **GROUP WORK** Ask questions about the people in the picture.

A: Is Bruce wearing a light brown jacket?
B: Yes, he is.
C: Is he wearing a tie?

C **GROUP WORK** Write five questions about your classmates. Then ask and answer the questions.

> Are Sonia and Paulo wearing jeans?
> Is Paulo wearing a red shirt?

11 INTERCHANGE 4 *Celebrity fashions*

What are your favorite celebrities wearing? Go to Interchange 4 on pages 116–117.

Units 3–4 Progress check

How well can you do these things? Check (✓) the boxes.

I can	Very well	OK	A little
Ask and answer questions about countries of origin, nationalities, and languages (Ex. 1)	☐	☐	☐
Understand descriptions of people (Ex. 2)	☐	☐	☐
Ask and answer questions about people's appearance and personality (Ex. 2, 5)	☐	☐	☐
Ask and answer questions about people's possessions (Ex. 3)	☐	☐	☐
Talk and write about my and other people's favorite things (Ex. 4)	☐	☐	☐
Ask and answer questions about what people are wearing (Ex. 5)	☐	☐	☐

1 INTERVIEW

Match the questions with the answers. Then ask and answer the
questions with a partner. Answer with your own information.

1. Are you from Malaysia? ....h......
2. Where are you and your family from? ....
3. What is your hometown like? ....
4. Is English your first language? ....
5. Who is your best friend? ....
6. Are your classmates Brazilian? ....
7. How old is your best friend? ....
8. Is our teacher from the U.S.? ....

a. It's very beautiful.
b. Yes, she is.
c. We're from Mexico.
d. My best friend is Kevin.
e. Yes, they are.
f. No, it's not. It's Spanish.
g. He's nineteen.
h. No, I'm not. I'm from Thailand.

2 LISTENING Who's that?

A ▶ Listen to four conversations. Check (✓) the correct description
for each person. You will check more than one adjective.

1. Min-ho	☐ tall	☐ short	☐ funny	☐ friendly	☐ talkative	☐ quiet
2. Ryan	☐ tall	☐ short	☐ funny	☐ serious	☐ friendly	☐ shy
3. Angela	☐ thin	☐ heavy	☐ pretty	☐ shy	☐ nice	☐ friendly
4. Helen	☐ thin	☐ heavy	☐ quiet	☐ shy	☐ serious	☐ funny

B Write five yes/no questions about the people in part A.
Then ask a partner the questions.

Is Min-ho friendly?
Is Ryan tall?

3 WHOSE CLOTHES ARE THESE?

CLASS ACTIVITY Draw three pictures of clothes on different pieces of paper. Then put the papers in a bag. Take three different papers, go around the class, and find the owners.

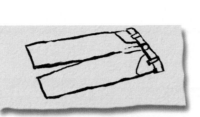

A: Gina, is this your cap?
B: No, it's not mine. Maybe it's Emi's.

A: Young-woo, are these your pants?
B: Yes, they're mine. Thanks!

4 MY FAVORITE THINGS

A Write your favorite things in the chart. Then ask a partner about his or her favorite things. Write them in the chart.

Favorite	Me	My partner
1. season	....	....
2. color	....	....
3. clothes	....	....

B Compare answers. What's the same? What's different? Write sentences.

> Summer is my favorite season, and it's Kyle's favorite season. That's the same.
> My favorite color is blue, but Kyle's favorite color is brown, so that's different.

5 GUESS THE CLASSMATE

GROUP WORK Think of a student in the class. Your classmates ask yes/no questions to guess the student.

A: I'm thinking of a student in this class.
B: Is it a man?
A: Yes, it is.
C: Is he short?
A: No, he isn't.
D: Is he wearing blue jeans?

WHAT'S NEXT?

Look at your Self-assessment again. Do you need to review anything?

5 What are you doing?

1 SNAPSHOT

▶ Listen and practice.

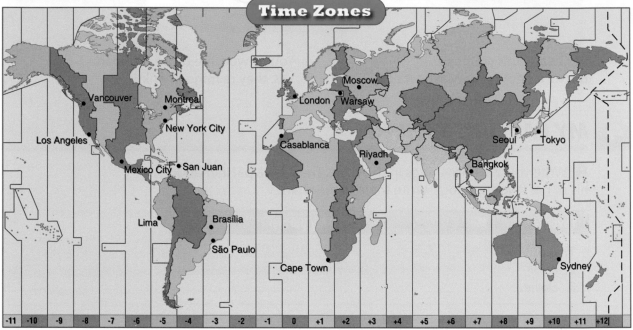

Time Zones

Source: Time Service Department, U.S. Naval Observatory

Which cities are in the same time zones?
Which cities are in your time zone?

2 CONVERSATION *What time is it there?*

▶ Listen and practice.

Debbie: Hello?
John: Hi, Debbie. This is John.
I'm calling from Australia.
Debbie: Australia?
John: I'm at a conference in Sydney.
Remember?
Debbie: Oh, right. What time is it there?
John: It's 10:00 P.M. And it's four o'clock
there in Los Angeles. Right?
Debbie: Yes – four o'clock in the morning!
John: 4:00 A.M.? Oh, I'm really sorry.
Debbie: That's OK. I'm awake . . . now.

30

What time is it? ▶

It's one **o'clock**.

It's one-oh-five.
It's five **after** one.

It's one-fifteen.
It's **a quarter after** one.

It's one-thirty.

It's one-forty.
It's twenty **to** two.

It's one forty-five.
It's **a quarter to** two.

A PAIR WORK Look at these clocks. What time is it?

1. 2. 3. 4. 5. 6.

A: What time is it?
B: It's twenty after two. OR It's two-twenty.

Is it A.M. **or** P.M.**?** ▶

It's seven (o'clock)
in the morning.
It's 7:00 A.M.

It's twelve (o'clock).
It's 12:00 P.M.
It's **noon**.

It's four (o'clock)
in the afternoon.
It's 4:00 P.M.

It's seven (o'clock)
in the evening.
It's 7:00 P.M.

It's ten (o'clock) **at night**.
It's 10:00 P.M.

It's twelve (o'clock) **at night**.
It's 12:00 A.M.
It's **midnight**.

B PAIR WORK Say each time a different way.

1. It's nine o'clock in the evening. *"It's 9:00 P.M."*
2. It's eight o'clock in the morning.
3. It's twelve o'clock at night.
4. It's three in the afternoon.

5. It's 3:00 A.M.
6. It's 6:00 P.M.
7. It's 4:00 P.M.
8. It's 12:00 P.M.

4 LISTENING *It's 4:00 P.M. in Vancouver.*

 Tracy and Eric are calling friends in different parts of the world. Listen. What time is it in these cities?

City	Time
Vancouver	4:00 p.m.
Bangkok	....
London	....
Tokyo	....
São Paulo	....

5 CONVERSATION *I'm really hungry!*

Listen and practice.

Steve: Hi, Mom.
Mom: What are you doing, Steve?
Steve: I'm cooking.
Mom: Why are you cooking now? It's two o'clock in the morning!
Steve: Well, I'm really hungry!
Mom: What are you making?
Steve: Pizza.
Mom: Oh? What kind?
Steve: Cheese and mushroom.
Mom: That's my favorite! Now I'm getting hungry. Let's eat!

6 PRONUNCIATION *Rising and falling intonation*

A ⊙ Listen and practice. Notice the intonation of the yes/no and Wh-questions.

Is she getting up? ⤴
Are they sleeping?

What's she doing? ⤵
What are they doing?

B ⊙ Listen to the questions. Draw a rising arrow (⤴) for rising intonation and a falling arrow (⤵) for falling intonation.

1. ⤴ 2. .... 3. .... 4. .... 5. .... 6. ....

GRAMMAR FOCUS *Present continuous Wh-questions* ▶

Los Angeles   4:00 A.M.

What's Victoria **doing**?
She**'s sleeping** right now.

Mexico City   6:00 A.M.

What's Marcos **doing**?
It's 6:00 A.M., so he**'s getting up.**

New York City   7:00 A.M.

What are Sue and Tom **doing**?
They**'re having** breakfast.

Brasília   9:00 A.M.

What's Célia **doing**?
She**'s going** to work.

London   12:00 noon

What are Jim and Ann **doing**?
It's noon, so they**'re eating** lunch.

Moscow   3:00 P.M.

What's Andrei **doing**?
He**'s working.**

Bangkok   7:00 P.M.

What's Permsak **doing**?
He**'s eating** dinner right now.

Tokyo   9:00 P.M.

What's Hiroshi **doing**?
He**'s checking** his email.

Your city   00:00

What are you **doing**?
It's . . . . I**'m** . . .

A **PAIR WORK** Ask and answer the questions about the pictures.

1. Who's sleeping now?
2. Who's having breakfast?
3. Where's Andrei working?
4. Where's Hiroshi checking his email?
5. What's Célia wearing?
6. What's Marcos wearing?
7. Why is Marcos getting up?
8. Why are Jim and Ann having lunch?

spelling
sleep ⟶ sleep**ing**
get ⟶ get**ting** (+ *t*)
have ⟶ hav**ing** (– *e*)

B **GROUP WORK** Write five more questions about the pictures.
Then ask and answer your questions in groups.

WORD POWER *Activities*

A ▶ Listen and practice. *"She's playing tennis."*

play tennis	ride a bike	run	swim
take a walk	dance	drive	watch a movie
shop	read	study	watch television

B **PAIR WORK** Ask and answer questions about the pictures in part A.

A: Is she playing soccer?
B: No, she's not.
A: What's she doing?
B: She's playing tennis.

C ▶ What's Mary doing? Listen to the sounds and number the actions from 1 to 8.

☐ dancing	☐ eating dinner	☐ riding a bike	☐ swimming
1 driving	☐ playing tennis	☐ shopping	☐ watching television

9

INTERCHANGE 5 *What's wrong with this picture?*

What's wrong with this picture? Go to Interchange 5 on page 119.

Friends Across a Continent

Skim the conversation. Write the name of the correct person under each picture.

Meg Martin and Kathy O'Brien chat online almost every day. Meg is an exchange student from the U.S. She's studying in Mexico. Kathy is in the U.S.

megm:	Hi, there!

kathyo:	Hi, Meg!

megm:	What are you doing?

kathyo:	I'm sitting on my bed with my laptop. I'm doing my homework.

megm:	What are you working on?

kathyo:	I'm writing an essay for Spanish class. :) Where are you?

megm:	I'm in a café with my friend Carmen. I'm having coffee, and she's talking on the phone outside. How is your family?

kathyo:	They're all fine! My father's watching a baseball game with his friends. My mother is out shopping.

megm:	Where's your brother?

kathyo:	John's playing soccer in the park. Oh, wait. My phone is ringing. My mother's calling me. I have to go! Bye!

megm:	OK! Bye!

_____

_____

A Read the conversation. Who is doing these things? Complete the sentences.

1. .... is writing an essay.
2. .... is having coffee.
3. .... is talking on the phone.
4. .... is watching a baseball game.
5. .... is shopping.
6. .... is playing soccer.

B **PAIR WORK** Imagine you are texting or chatting online. Where are you? Who are you communicating with? Write a short conversation.

6 My sister works downtown.

SNAPSHOT

▶ Listen and practice.

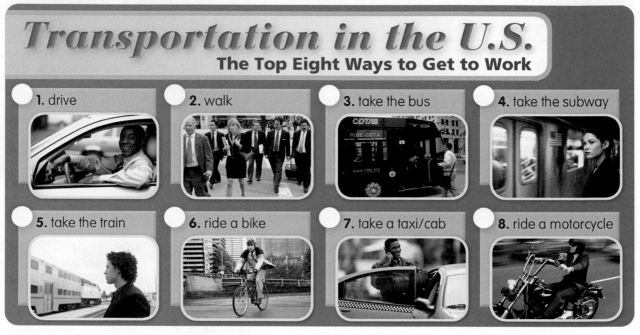

Transportation in the U.S.
The Top Eight Ways to Get to Work

1. drive
2. walk
3. take the bus
4. take the subway
5. take the train
6. ride a bike
7. take a taxi/cab
8. ride a motorcycle

Source: U.S. Census Bureau

Check (✓) the kinds of transportation you use.
What are some other kinds of transportation?

2 **CONVERSATION** *Nice car!*

▶ Listen and practice.

Ashley: Nice car, Jason! Is it yours?

Jason: No, it's my sister's. She has a new job, and she drives to work.

Ashley: Is her job here in the suburbs?

Jason: No, it's downtown.

Ashley: My parents work downtown, but they don't drive to work. They use public transportation.

Jason: The bus or the train?

Ashley: The train doesn't stop near our house, so they take the bus.

3 WORD POWER *Family*

A ▶ **PAIR WORK** Complete the sentences about the Carter family. Then listen and check your answers.

1. Anne is Paul's ......*wife*...... .
2. Jason and Emily are their ....
3. Paul is Anne's ....
4. Jason is Anne's ....
5. Emily is Paul's ....
6. Jason is Emily's ....
7. Emily is Jason's ....
8. Paul and Anne are Jason's ....

| husband | wife |

Paul · Anne

| father | mother |
| (parents) | |

| son | daughter |
| (children) | |

| brother | sister |

Jason · Emily

> kids = children
> mom = mother
> dad = father

B **PAIR WORK** Who are the people in your family? What are their names?

"My mother's name is Angela. My brothers' names are David and Daniel."

4 GRAMMAR FOCUS

Simple present statements ▶

I **walk**	to school.	I **don't live**	far from here.	**don't** = do not
You **ride**	your bike to school.	You **don't live**	near here.	**doesn't** = does not
He **works**	near here.	He **doesn't work**	downtown.	
She **takes**	the bus to work.	She **doesn't drive**	to work.	
We **live**	with our parents.	We **don't live**	alone.	
They **use**	public transportation.	They **don't need**	a car.	

A Paul Carter is talking about his family. Complete the sentences with the correct verb forms. Then compare with a partner.

1. My family and I ......*live*...... (live / lives) in the suburbs. My wife and I .... (work / works) near here, so we .... (walk / walks) to work. Our daughter Emily .... (work / works) downtown, so she .... (drive / drives) to work. Our son .... (don't / doesn't) drive. He .... (ride / rides) his bike to school.

2. My parents .... (live / lives) in the city. My mother .... (take / takes) a train to work. My father is retired, so he .... (don't / doesn't) work now. He also .... (use / uses) public transportation, so they .... (don't / doesn't) need a car.

verb endings: *he, she, it*
walk ⟶ walk**s**
ride ⟶ ride**s**
study ⟶ stud**ies**
watch ⟶ watch**es**

My sister works downtown. ▪ **37**

B Ashley is talking about her family and her friend Jason.
Complete the sentences. Then compare with a partner.

1. My parents ......*have*...... (have / has) a house in the suburbs. My mom
   and dad .... (go / goes) downtown to work. My parents are very
   busy, so I .... (do / does) a lot of work at home.

2. My brother doesn't live with us. He .... (have / has) an apartment in
   the city. He .... (go / goes) to school all day, and he .... (do / does)
   his homework at night.

3. I .... (have / has) a new friend. His name is Jason. We ....
   (go / goes) to the same school, and sometimes we .... (do / does)
   our homework together.

C **PAIR WORK** Tell your partner about your family.

"I have one brother and two sisters. My brother is a teacher.
He has a car, so he drives to work."

---

5 **PRONUNCIATION** *Third-person singular -s endings*

⊙ Listen and practice. Notice the pronunciation of the **-s** endings.

s = /s/	s = /z/	(e)s = /ɪz/	*irregular*
take take**s**	drive drive**s**	dance dance**s**	do do**es**
sleep sleep**s**	study stud**ies**	watch watch**es**	have ha**s**

---

6 **CONVERSATION** *I get up at noon.*

⊙ Listen and practice.

Jack: Let's go to the park on Sunday.
Amy: OK, but let's go in the afternoon.
     I sleep late on weekends.
Jack: What time do you get up on Sundays?
Amy: At ten o'clock.
Jack: Oh, that's early. On Sundays,
     I get up at noon.
Amy: Really? Do you eat breakfast then?
Jack: Sure. I have breakfast every day.
Amy: Then let's meet at this restaurant at
     one o'clock. They serve breakfast all day!

Simple present questions ▶

Do you **get up** early?	**What time do** you **get up**?
No, I **get up** late.	At ten o'clock.
Does he **eat** lunch at noon?	**What time does** he **have** dinner?
No, he **eats** lunch at one o'clock.	At eight o'clock.
Do they **take** the bus to class?	**When do** they **take** the subway?
No, they **take** the subway.	On Tuesdays and Thursdays.

A Complete the questions with *do* or *does*.

1. ......Do...... you get up early on weekdays?
2. What time .... you go home on Fridays?
3. .... your father work on weekends?
4. .... your mother cook every day?
5. .... your parents read in the evening?
6. When .... your parents shop?
7. .... you check your email at night?
8. What time .... you have dinner?
9. When .... you study?
10. .... your best friend drive to class?
11. What time .... your father get up?

time expressions	
early	**in** the morning
late	**in** the afternoon
every day	**in** the evening
at 9:00	**on** Sundays
at noon / midnight	**on** weekdays
at night	**on** weekends

B **PAIR WORK** Ask and answer the questions from part A. Use time expressions from the box.

A: Do you get up early on weekdays?
B: Yes. I get up at seven o'clock.

C Unscramble the questions to complete the conversations. Then ask a partner the questions. Answer with your own information.

1. A: Do you check your email every day .... ?
      you / every day / check your email / do
   B: Yes, I check my email every day.

2. A: .... ?
      you / what time / lunch / do / eat
   B: At 1:00 P.M.

3. A: .... ?
      at / start / does / eight o'clock / this class
   B: No, this class starts at nine o'clock.

4. A: .... ?
      study / you / English / do / when
   B: I study English in the evening.

5. A: .... ?
      on weekends / you and your friends / do / play sports
   B: Yes, we play soccer on Saturdays.

8 LISTENING *Marsha's weekly routine*

Listen to Marsha talk about her weekly routine.
Check (✓) the days she does each thing.

	Monday	Tuesday	Wednesday	Thursday	Friday	Saturday	Sunday
get up early	☐	☐	☐	☐	☐	☐	☐
go to work	☐	☐	☐	☐	☐	☐	☐
exercise	☐	☐	☐	☐	☐	☐	☐
see friends	☐	☐	☐	☐	☐	☐	☐
see family	☐	☐	☐	☐	☐	☐	☐
study	☐	☐	☐	☐	☐	☐	☐

9 MY ROUTINE

A What do you do every week? Write things in the chart.

	Calendar					
Sunday	**Monday**	**Tuesday**	**Wednesday**	**Thursday**	**Friday**	**Saturday**

◀ Day Week Month ▶

B **GROUP WORK** Discuss your weekly routines. Ask and
answer questions.

A: I go to bed late on Fridays.
B: What do you do on Friday nights?
A: I see my friends. We watch television or play
   video games.
C: On Fridays, I study in the evening. I see my friends
   on the weekend.

10 INTERCHANGE 6 *Class survey*

Find out more about your classmates. Go to Interchange 6 on page 120.

What's your schedule like?

Look at the pictures and the labels. Who gets up early? Who gets up late?

Student reporter Mike Starr talks to people on the street about their schedules.

Brittany Davis
College Student

Mike: **What's your schedule like?**
Brittany: My classes start at 8:00 A.M., so I get up at 7:00 and take the bus to school.
MS: **When do your classes end?**
BD: They end at noon. Then I have a job at the library.
MS: **So when do you study?**
BD: My only time to study is in the evening, from eight until midnight.

Justin Reid
City Tour Guide

Mike: **What's your schedule like?**
Justin: I get up at 6:15 A.M. and start work at 9:00.
MS: **And what do you do before work?**
JR: I go for a run at 6:30 A.M., and then I have breakfast at 7:00.
MS: **And after work?**
JR: I finish at 6:00 P.M., and I have dinner downtown.
MS: **Do you work every day?**
JR: No, I work on Fridays, Saturdays, and Sundays.

Maya Choo
Rock Musician

Mike: **What's your schedule like?**
Maya: Well, I work at night. I go to work at 10:00 P.M., and I play until 3:00 A.M.
MS: **What do you do after work?**
MC: I have dinner at 3:30 or 4:00. Then I take a taxi home.
MS: **What time do you go to bed?**
MC: I go to bed at 5:00 in the morning.

A Read the article. Then number the activities in each person's schedule from 1 to 5.

Brittany Davis
.... a. She goes to class.
.... b. She takes the bus.
.... c. She works.
.... d. She studies.
...1... e. She gets up.

Justin Reid
.... a. He has breakfast.
.... b. He starts work.
.... c. He eats dinner.
.... d. He gets up.
.... e. He goes for a run.

Maya Choo
.... a. She has dinner.
.... b. She finishes work.
.... c. She goes to bed.
.... d. She goes to work.
.... e. She goes home.

B Write five sentences about your schedule. Are you an "early bird" or a "night owl"? Compare with a partner.

early bird

night owl

Units 5–6 Progress check

How well can you do these things? Check (✓) the boxes.

I can	Very well	OK	A little
Understand times and descriptions of activities (Ex. 1)	☐	☐	☐
Ask and answer questions about present activities (Ex. 2)	☐	☐	☐
Talk about personal routines (Ex. 3)	☐	☐	☐
Ask and answer questions about routines (Ex. 4)	☐	☐	☐
Ask and answer questions about people's lifestyles and appearance (Ex. 5)	☐	☐	☐

1 LISTENING *Around the world*

 It's 9 A.M. in Los Angeles. Vanessa is calling friends around the world. Listen to the conversations and complete the chart.

	City	Time	Activity
1. Sarah	New York	....	....
2. Manuel	....	....	....
3. Bob	....	....	....

2 ON VACATION

Student A: Imagine your classmates are on vacation. Student B calls you. Ask questions about your classmates.

Student B: Imagine you are on vacation with your classmates. Call Student A. Answer Student A's questions about your classmates.

A: Hello?
B: Hi, it's . . . . I'm on vacation in . . .
A: In . . . ? Wow! What are you doing?
B: . . .
A: Who are you with?
B: . . .
A: What's he/she doing?
B: . . .
A: Well, have fun. Bye!

3 MY DAILY ROUTINE

A Choose one day of the week and write it in the blank.
What do you do on this day? Complete the chart.

	Day ....
In the morning	....
In the afternoon	....
In the evening	....
At night	....

B **PAIR WORK** Tell your partner about your routine.

A: On Saturdays, I exercise in the morning. I play soccer with my friends.
B: What time do you play?
A: We play at 10:00.

4 LIFESTYLE SURVEY

A Answer the questions in the chart. Check (✓) Yes or No.

	Yes	No	Name
1. Do you live with your parents?	☐	☐	....
2. Do both your parents work?	☐	☐	....
3. Do you watch television at night?	☐	☐	....
4. Do you eat dinner with your family?	☐	☐	....
5. Do you stay home on weekends?	☐	☐	....
6. Do you work on Saturdays?	☐	☐	....

B **CLASS ACTIVITY** Go around the class and find classmates with the same answers.
Write their names in the chart. Try to write a different name on each line.

5 WHO IS IT?

GROUP WORK Think of a famous person. Your classmates
ask yes/no questions to guess the person.

Is it a man? a woman?   Is he/she tall? short?
Does he/she live in . . . ?   Does he/she wear glasses?
Is he/she a singer? an actor?

WHAT'S NEXT?

Look at your Self-assessment again. Do you need to review anything?

7 Does it have a view?

SNAPSHOT

▶ Listen and practice.

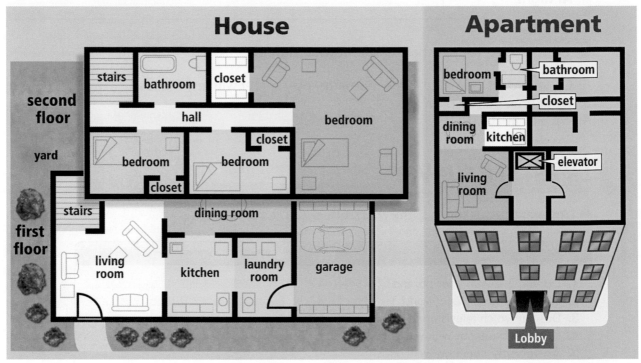

Source: www.floorplanner.com

What rooms are in houses in your country? What rooms are in apartments?
What rooms are in your house or apartment?

2 ## CONVERSATION *My new apartment*

▶ Listen and practice.

Linda: Guess what! I have a new apartment.
Chris: That's great! What's it like?
Linda: It's really nice.
Chris: Is it very big?
Linda: Well, it has a big living room, a bedroom, a bathroom, and a kitchen.
Chris: Nice! Do you live downtown?
Linda: No, I don't. I live near the university.
Chris: Does it have a view?
Linda: Yes, it does. It has a great view of another apartment building!

> **Simple present short answers** ▶
>
> **Do** you **live** in an apartment?
>   Yes, I **do**. / No, I **don't**.
> **Do** the bedrooms **have** windows?
>   Yes, they **do**. / No, they **don't**.
>
> **Does** Chris **live** in a house?
>   Yes, he **does**. / No, he **doesn't**.
> **Does** the house **have** a yard?
>   Yes, it **does**. / No, it **doesn't**.

A Complete the conversation. Then practice with a partner.

Linda: ____Do____ you ____live____ in an apartment?
Chris: No, I _____ . I _____ in a house.
Linda: _____ it _____ a yard?
Chris: Yes, it _____ .
Linda: That sounds nice. _____ you _____ alone?
Chris: No, I _____ . I _____ with my family.
Linda: _____ you _____ any brothers or sisters?
Chris: Yes, I _____ . I _____ four sisters.
Linda: Really? _____ your house _____ many bedrooms?
Chris: Yes, it _____ . It _____ four.
Linda: _____ you _____ your own bedroom?
Chris: Yes, I _____ . I'm really lucky.

B **PAIR WORK** Read the conversation in part A again. Ask and answer these questions about Chris.

1. Does he live in an apartment?
2. Does his house have a yard?

3. Does he live alone?
4. Does he have his own room?

C **PAIR WORK** Write five questions to ask your partner about his or her home. Then ask and answer the questions.

4 **LISTENING** *It has just one room.*

▶ Listen to four people describe their homes. Number the pictures from 1 to 4.

WORD POWER *Furniture*

A ▶ Listen and practice.

| armchairs | stove | curtains | pictures | bed |

| table | coffee table | microwave oven | refrigerator | lamps |

| sofa | desk | bookcase | dresser | chairs |

| mirror | rug | TV | cupboards |

B Which rooms have the things in part A? Complete the chart.

Kitchen	table stove
Dining room	table
Living room	
Bedroom	

C **GROUP WORK** What furniture is in your house or apartment? Tell your classmates.

"My living room has a sofa, a rug, and a TV. . . ."

6 CONVERSATION *There aren't any chairs.*

Listen and practice.

Chris: This apartment is great.
Linda: Thanks. I love it, but I really need some furniture.
Chris: What do you need?
Linda: Oh, I need lots of things. There are some chairs in the kitchen, but there isn't a table.
Chris: And there's no sofa here in the living room.
Linda: And there aren't any chairs. There's only this lamp.
Chris: So let's go shopping next weekend.

7 GRAMMAR FOCUS

> ### There is, there are
>
> | | | |
> |---|---|---|
> | **There's a** bed in the bedroom. | **There are some** chairs in the kitchen. | **There's** = There is |
> | **There's no** sofa in the bedroom. | **There are no** chairs in the living room. | |
> | **There isn't a** table in the kitchen. | **There aren't any** chairs in the living room. | |

A Look at the picture of Linda's apartment. Complete the sentences. Then practice with a partner.

1. ....*There's no*.... dresser in the bedroom.
2. .... chairs in the kitchen.
3. .... TV in the living room.
4. .... refrigerator.
5. .... rugs on the floor.
6. .... curtains on the windows.
7. .... mirror in the bedroom.
8. .... books in the bookcase.

B Write five sentences about things you have or don't have in your classroom. Then compare with a partner.

There are 10 desks in the classroom.

8 INTERCHANGE 7 *Find the differences*

Compare two apartments. Go to Interchange 7 on page 121.

Does it have a view? ▪ **47**

9 PRONUNCIATION *Words with th*

A ▶ Listen and practice. Notice the pronunciation of /θ/ and /ð/.

/ð/   /θ/   /ð/   /ð/   /θ/   /θ/

There are **th**irteen rooms in **th**is house. **The** house has **th**ree ba**th**rooms.

B **PAIR WORK** List other words with /θ/ and /ð/. Then use them to write four funny sentences. Read them aloud.

> On Thursdays, their mother and father think for thirteen minutes.

10 LISTENING *Furniture is expensive!*

▶ Listen to Chris and Linda talk in a furniture store. What does Linda like? Check (✓) the things.

☐ armchairs   ☐ a sofa   ☐ a rug   ☐ lamps
☐ a bookcase   ☐ a mirror   ☐ a coffee table   ☐ curtains

11 MY DREAM HOME

A Write a description of your dream home.

What is your dream home like?
Where is it?
What rooms does it have?
What things are in the rooms?
Does it have a view?

> My dream home is a loft in a big city. There is one large living room with a lot of windows. There are two bedrooms and . . .

loft

cabin

villa

beach house

B **PAIR WORK** Ask your partner about his or her dream home.

A: Does it have a view?
B: Yes, it has a very nice view of the forest. . . .

Unusual Homes

Scan the article. Where are the lofts? Where does Dan Phillips build houses?

🏠 Shusaku Arakawa and Madeline Gins are famous designers. Their nine lofts near Tokyo, Japan, are very colorful. The apartments are blue, pink, red, yellow, and other bright colors. Inside, the walls are colorful, too. The floors go up and down, and some rooms are round. The windows have strange shapes, so there are no curtains. There are small doors to the outside. Inside, there aren't any closets. The bookcase is in the middle of the living room.

🏠 Dan Phillips likes to help people. He builds houses for artists and other low-income people in Huntsville, Texas, in the United States. One house, the "tree house," is in a large tree in the forest. It has windows on the floor! It also has a small kitchen. The bed is on the upstairs floor. There is a wood-burning stove from an old ship in the living room. Phillips teaches people how to build houses with recycled materials.

A Read the article. What's in each home? Complete the chart.

bed on the upstairs floor	bookcase	closets
✓ colorful walls	windows on the floor	wood-burning stove

Arakawa and Gins's lofts	Dan Phillips's tree house
1. There are _colorful walls_ .	**4.** There are ....
2. There aren't any	**5.** There is a ....
3. There is a .... in the middle of the living room.	**6.** There is a ....

B **GROUP WORK** Talk about these questions.

1. Imagine you are painting your house. What colors do you use? Why?
2. Imagine you are building a house. Do you use new materials or recycled materials? Why?

8 What do you do?

1 WORD POWER Jobs

A ▶ Match the jobs with the pictures. Then listen and practice.

a. accountant	e. electrician	i. painter	m. salesperson
b. bellhop	f. front desk clerk	j. plumber	n. security guard
c. cashier	g. nurse	✓k. police officer	o. taxi driver
d. doctor	h. office manager	l. receptionist	p. vendor

1. k   2.   3.

4.   5.   6.

7.   8.   9.

10.   11.

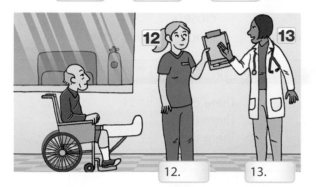

12.   13.

14.   15.   16.

B **PAIR WORK** Ask questions about the people in part A. What are their jobs?

A: What's her job?
B: She's a police officer.

2 THE WORKPLACE

A **PAIR WORK** Who works in these places? Complete the chart with jobs from Exercise 1. Add one more job to each list.

A: A doctor works in a hospital.
B: A nurse works in a hospital, too.

In a hospital	In an office	In a store	In a hotel
doctor			
nurse			

B **CLASS ACTIVITY** Ask and answer *Who* questions about jobs. Use these words.

wears a uniform	sits all day	talks to people	works hard
stands all day	handles money	works at night	makes a lot of money

A: Who wears a uniform?
B: A police officer wears a uniform.
C: And a security guard . . .

3 CONVERSATION *He works in a hotel.*

▶ Listen and practice.

Rachel: Where does your brother work?
Angela: In a hotel.
Rachel: Oh, really? My brother works in a hotel, too. He's a front desk clerk.
Angela: How does he like it?
Rachel: He hates it. He doesn't like the manager.
Angela: That's too bad. What hotel does he work for?
Rachel: The Plaza.
Angela: That's funny. My brother works there, too.
Rachel: Oh, that's interesting. What does he do?
Angela: Actually, he's the manager!

GRAMMAR FOCUS

> ## Simple present Wh-questions ▶
>
> | | | |
> |---|---|---|
> | **Where do** you **work?** | **Where does** he **work?** | **Where do** they **work?** |
> | In a hospital. | In a hotel. | In a store. |
> | **What do** you **do?** | **What does** he **do?** | **What do** they **do?** |
> | I'm a doctor. | He's a manager. | They're cashiers. |
> | **How do** you **like** it? | **How does** he **like** it? | **How do** they **like** it? |
> | I really like it. | It's OK. | They hate it. |

A Complete these conversations. Then practice with a partner.

1. A: ....*What*.... does your sister ....*do*.... ?
   B: My sister? She's a nurse.
   A: .... does she .... it?
   B: It's difficult, but she loves it.

2. A: .... does your brother .... ?
   B: In a hotel. He's a front desk clerk.
   A: Oh? .... does he .... it?
   B: He doesn't really like it.

3. A: .... do your parents .... their jobs?
   B: Oh, I guess they like them.
   A: I don't remember. .... do they .... ?
   B: In an office in the city.

4. A: .... do you .... ?
   B: I'm a student.
   A: I see. .... do you .... your classes?
   B: They're great. I like them a lot.

B **PAIR WORK** Ask questions about these people.
Where do they work? What do they do? How do they like it?

David	Laura	Brian and Jessica

A: Where does David work?
B: He works in . . .

5 PRONUNCIATION *Reduction of* do

▶ Listen and practice. Notice the reduction of **do**.

Where **do you** work?   Where **do they** work?

What **do you** do?   What **do they** do?

6 SNAPSHOT

▶ Listen and practice.

What do you do? What's your job like?

I'm a server in a coffee shop. It's easy, but boring. I don't like my job much.

I'm a firefighter. It's exciting and very dangerous, but I like my job a lot.

I'm a social worker. It's difficult and really stressful, but I love my job.

I'm a florist. My job isn't very exciting, but it's pretty relaxing. I like my job OK.

Source: www.careercast.com

Who likes his or her job? Who doesn't? Why or why not?
How do they describe their jobs? Write one more adjective for each job.

7 CONVERSATION *Please be careful!*

▶ Listen and practice.

Richard: Hey, Stephanie. I hear you have a new job.
Stephanie: Yes. I'm teaching math at Lincoln High School.
Richard: How do you like it?
Stephanie: It's great. The students are terrific. How are things with you?
Richard: Not bad. I'm a window washer now, you know.
Stephanie: Really? How do you like it?
Richard: It's a stressful job. And it's pretty dangerous.
Stephanie: Please be careful!

8 LISTENING *It's pretty boring.*

▶ Listen to four people talk about their jobs. Complete the chart with the correct jobs and adjectives.

	What do you do?	What's it like?
1. Monica		
2. Hye-soon		
3. Kirk		
4. Philip		

What do you do? ■ **53**

9 GRAMMAR FOCUS

Placement of adjectives ⏵

be + adjective	adjective + noun
A doctor's job **is stressful**.	A doctor has **a stressful job**.
A window washer's job **is dangerous**.	A window washer has **a dangerous job**.

A Write each sentence a different way. Then compare with a partner.

1. A doctor's job is interesting. <u>A doctor has an interesting job.</u>
2. A police officer's job is dangerous. ....
3. A teacher's job is stressful. ....
4. A plumber has a boring job. ....
5. An electrician has a difficult job. ....
6. A vendor has an easy job. ....

B GROUP WORK Write one job for each adjective.
Do your classmates agree?

flight attendant

1. exciting <u>flight attendant</u>	**4.** boring ....
2. easy	**5.** difficult ....
3. dangerous	**6.** relaxing ....

A: A flight attendant has an exciting job.
B: I don't agree. A flight attendant's job is boring.
C: I think . . .

10 INTERCHANGE 8 *The perfect job*

What do you want in a job? Go to Interchange 8 on page 122.

11 WORKDAY ROUTINES

GROUP WORK Ask three classmates about their jobs (or their
friends' or family members' jobs). Then tell the class.

Ask about a classmate
Do you have a job?
Where do you work?
What do you do, exactly?
Is your job interesting?
What time do you start work?
When do you finish work?
Do you like your job?
What do you do after work? . . .

**Ask about a classmate's
friend or family member**
Tell me about your . . .
Where does he/she work?
What does he/she do, exactly?
Is his/her job difficult?
What time does he/she start work?
When does he/she finish work?
Does he/she like his/her job?
What does he/she do after work? . . .

JOB Profiles

Look at the photos. Which jobs look interesting? Why?

dog groomer

Lots of **Marco Mendez**'s friends walk on four legs. He makes these furry friends beautiful. Marco is a professional dog groomer. He likes his job a lot because it's never boring. Each dog has a different personality. What's his favorite kind of dog? He's not telling!

wedding planner

Lila Martin goes to nice restaurants, eats cake, listens to bands – and gets paid for it! Lila is a wedding planner. She chooses the place, the food, and the music for people's weddings. It's stressful because everything needs to be perfect!

video game designer

Hal Garner has his dream job. He plays video games all day long! Hal is a game designer for a large video game company. He makes new games and tests them. It's always exciting, and he almost always wins!

baker

Junko Watanabe has a sweet life. She makes bread, cookies, and cakes in her neighborhood bakery. Junko really likes her job. Her salary isn't great, but the customers love her cakes and cookies, so she's happy.

A Read the article. Who says these things? Write your guesses.

1. "I go to work very early in the morning." ....
2. "I know every restaurant in town." ....
3. "After work, I need to take a bath!" ....
4. "I sit down all day long!" ....

B Write a short description of a job, but don't write the name of the job.
Then read it to the class. Your classmates guess the job.

Units 7–8 Progress check

SELF-ASSESSMENT

How well can you do these things? Check (✓) the boxes.

I can	Very well	OK	A little
Ask and answer questions about living spaces (Ex. 1)	☐	☐	☐
Talk about rooms and furniture (Ex. 1)	☐	☐	☐
Ask and answer questions about work (Ex. 2)	☐	☐	☐
Understand descriptions of jobs (Ex. 3)	☐	☐	☐
Give and respond to opinions about jobs (Ex. 4)	☐	☐	☐

1 A NEW APARTMENT

A Imagine you are moving into this apartment. What things are in the rooms? Draw pictures. Use the furniture in the box and your own ideas.

bed	desk	lamp	sofa
chairs	dresser	mirror	table

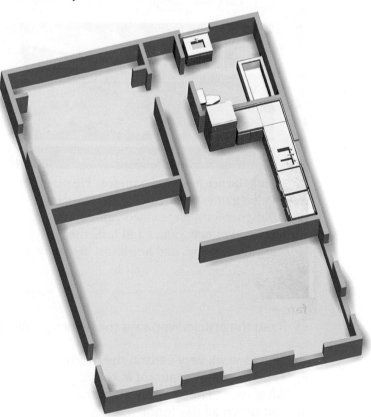

B **PAIR WORK** Ask questions about your partner's apartment.

A: I'm moving into a new apartment!
B: That's great! Where is it?
A: . . .
B: What's it like? Does it have many rooms?
A: Well, it has . . .
B: Does the . . . have . . . ?
A: . . .
B: Do you have a lot of furniture?
A: Well, there's . . . in the . . .
   There are some . . . in the . . .
B: Do you have everything you need for the apartment?
A: No, I don't. There's no . . .
   There isn't any . . .
   There aren't any . . .
B: OK. Let's go shopping this weekend!

WHERE DOES HE WORK?

A Complete the conversations with Wh-questions.

1. A: <u>Where does your father work</u>?
   B: My father? He works in a store.
   A: _____?
   B: He's a salesperson.
   A: _____?
   B: He likes his job a lot!

2. A: _____?
   B: I'm an accountant.
   A: _____?
   B: I work in an office.
   A: _____?
   B: It's OK. I guess I like it.

B **PAIR WORK** Your partner asks the questions in part A. Answer with your own information.

 3 **LISTENING** *Where do they work?*

⏵ Listen to Linda, Kyle, and Wendy talk about their jobs. Check (✓) the correct answers.

	Where do they work?		What do they do?	
1. Linda	☐ office	☐ store	☐ receptionist	☐ doctor
2. Kyle	☐ hospital	☐ school	☐ nurse	☐ teacher
3. Wendy	☐ hotel	☐ office	☐ manager	☐ bellhop

4 **AN INTERESTING JOB**

GROUP WORK What do you think of these jobs? Give your opinions.

farmer

bus driver

architect

hairstylist

A: I think a farmer has a boring job.
B: I don't really agree. I think a farmer's job is relaxing.
C: Well, I think a farmer's job is difficult. . . .

WHAT'S NEXT?

Look at your Self-assessment again. Do you need to review anything?

9 LISTENING *I can do that!*

Listen to three people talk about their abilities. Check (✓) the things they can do well.

1. Craig
2. Julie
3. Rob

10 WORD POWER

A Complete the word map with abilities and talents from the list.
Then listen and check.

- ✓ bake a cake
- download a video
- do yoga
- fix a car
- play chess
- play the violin
- ride a horse
- sing English songs
- snowboard
- tell good jokes
- upload photos
- write poems

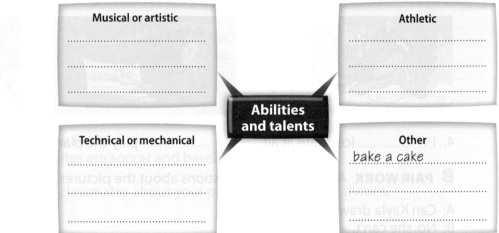

Musical or artistic

Athletic

Abilities and talents

Technical or mechanical

Other
bake a cake

B **GROUP WORK** Who can do the things in part A?
Make a list of guesses about your classmates.

A: Who can bake a cake?
B: I think Sophie can.
C: Who can download . . . ?

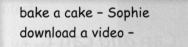
bake a cake – Sophie
download a video –

C **CLASS ACTIVITY** Go around the room and check your guesses.

A: Sophie, can you bake a cake?
B: Yes, I can.

11 INTERCHANGE 10 *Hidden talents*

Learn more about your classmates' hidden talents. Go to Interchange 10 on page 124.

An interview with Shawn Johnson

How often do you think professional athletes practice?

Get a sneak peek inside the life of this U.S. gold medal–winning Olympic gymnast!

Where are you from?

Des Moines, Iowa. I live there now.

Who do you train with?

A lot of people think I have a private coach. But I train with 13 other girls at the gym!

How often do you practice?

Most athletes train about 45 hours a week. But my parents want me to have a "normal life." I train about 25 hours a week. I usually work out four hours a day during the week, and five to six hours on Saturdays. I don't practice on Sundays.

What do you eat to stay healthy?

I have to watch my diet to be a healthy gymnast. But I don't get stressed about it.

What are your favorite foods?

Chicken and steak kebabs, peaches and cream, and corn on the cob.

What do you do when you're not training?

I love to ride horses and spend time with my friends.

What do you do for good luck?

I always travel with my blankets. But I don't believe in good-luck charms!

Who are your biggest fans?

My mom, dad, and of course my coach!

A Read the interview. Then check (✓) the correct answers to the questions.

1. Who does Shawn train with?
   a. ☐ just her coach   b. ☐ other gymnasts

2. How often does she practice?
   a. ☐ 25 hours a week   b. ☐ 45 hours a week

3. How much does she train on Saturdays?
   a. ☐ four hours   b. ☐ five to six hours

4. What does she like to do in her free time?
   a. ☐ eat in restaurants   b. ☐ ride horses and be with friends

5. What does she travel with?
   a. ☐ a good-luck charm   b. ☐ her blankets

B GROUP WORK Do you think athletes have an easy life? Is playing a sport fun, or hard work? Discuss your reasons with your classmates.

11 What are you going to do?

1 MONTHS AND DATES

A ▶ Listen and practice the months.

Months	January	February	March	April	May	June
	July	August	September	October	November	December

B ▶ Complete the dates. Then listen and practice.

Dates					
1st	first	11th	eleventh	21st	twenty-first
2nd	second		twelfth		twenty-second
	third	13th	thirteenth	23rd	twenty-third
4th	fourth	14th	fourteenth		twenty-fourth
5th	fifth		fifteenth	25th	twenty-fifth
6th	sixth	16th	sixteenth		twenty-sixth
	seventh	17th	seventeenth	27th	twenty-seventh
8th	eighth	18th	eighteenth		twenty-eighth
9th	ninth		nineteenth	29th	twenty-ninth
	tenth	20th	twentieth		thirtieth
					thirty-first

C CLASS ACTIVITY Go around the room. Ask your classmates' birthdays.

A: When's your birthday?
B: It's July twenty-first. When's yours?

2 CONVERSATION *Birthday plans*

▶ Listen and practice.

Angie: Are you going to do anything exciting this weekend?
Philip: Well, I'm going to celebrate my birthday.
Angie: Oh, happy birthday! When is it, exactly?
Philip: It's August ninth – Sunday.
Angie: So what are your plans?
Philip: I'm going to go to my friend Kayla's house.
She's going to cook a special dinner for me.
Angie: Nice! Is she going to bake a cake, too?
Philip: Bake a cake? Oh, I'm not sure.

GRAMMAR FOCUS

The future with be going to ▶

Are you **going to do** anything this weekend?	Yes, I am. I**'m going to celebrate** my birthday.
	No, I'm not. I**'m going to stay** home.
Is Kayla **going to cook** dinner for you?	Yes, she is. She**'s going to cook** a special dinner.
	No, she's not. She**'s going to order** takeout.
Are your friends **going to be** there?	Yes, they are. They**'re going to stop** by after dinner.
	No, they're not. They**'re going to be** away all weekend.

A What are these people going to do this weekend?
Write sentences. Then compare with a partner.

1. They're going to go dancing.

B **PAIR WORK** Is your partner going to do the things in part A
this weekend? Ask and answer questions.

"Are you going to go dancing this weekend?"

4 ## PRONUNCIATION *Reduction of* going to

A ▶ Listen and practice. Notice the reduction of **going to** to /gənə/.

A: Are you **going to** have a party?
B: No. I'm **going to** meet a friend.

A: Are you **going to** go to a restaurant?
B: Yes. We're **going to** go to Nick's Café.

B **PAIR WORK** Ask your partner about his or her evening plans. Try to reduce **going to**.

5 LISTENING *Evening plans*

A It's 5:30 P.M. What are these people's evening plans? Write your guesses in the chart.

B Listen to the interview. What are the people really going to do? Complete the chart.

Michelle   **Kevin**   **Robert**   **Jackie**

Your guess		What they're really going to do	
Michelle	*is going to go to the gym* .	Michelle	.
Kevin	.	Kevin	.
Robert	.	Robert	.
Jackie	.	Jackie	.

6 INTERCHANGE 11 *Guessing game*

Make guesses about your classmates' plans. Go to Interchange 11 on page 125.

7 SNAPSHOT

Listen and practice.

Holidays in the United States

New Year's Day — January 1st

Valentine's Day — February 14th

Independence Day — July 4th

Halloween — October 31st

Thanksgiving — The fourth Thursday in November

Christmas — December 25th

Source: *The Concise Columbia Encyclopedia*

Do you celebrate any of these holidays?
What are some holidays in your country? What's your favorite holiday?

8 CONVERSATION *Have a good Valentine's Day.*

▶ Listen and practice.

Mona: So, Tyler, do you have any plans for Valentine's Day?
Tyler: I do. I'm going to take my girlfriend out for dinner.
Mona: Oh, really? Where are you going to eat?
Tyler: At Laguna's. It's her favorite restaurant.
Mona: How fancy! She's going to like that!
Tyler: How about you? What are you going to do?
Mona: Well, I'm not going to go to a restaurant.
           I'm going to go to a dance.
Tyler: Sounds like fun. Well, have a good
           Valentine's Day.
Mona: Thanks. You, too.

9 GRAMMAR FOCUS

Wh-questions with be going to ▶

What are you **going to do** for Valentine's Day?	**I'm going to go** to a dance. **I'm not going to go** to a restaurant.
How is Mona **going to get** to the dance?	She**'s going to drive**. She**'s not going to take** the bus.
Where are Tyler and his girlfriend **going to eat**?	They**'re going to eat** at Laguna's. They**'re not going to eat** at Nick's Café.

A Complete these conversations with the correct form of *be going to*.
Then practice with a partner.

1. A: Where ......*are*...... you ....*going to spend*.... (spend) summer vacation?
   B: My parents and I .... (visit) my grandparents.
2. B: Who .... you .... (invite) to Thanksgiving dinner?
   A: I .... (ask) my family and some good friends.
3. A: What .... you .... (do) for Halloween?
   B: I don't know. I .... (not do) anything special.
4. A: How .... your parents .... (celebrate) New Year's Eve?
   B: They .... (go) to their neighbor's party.
5. A: What .... your sister .... (do) for her birthday?
   B: Her boyfriend .... (take) her out to dinner.

B **GROUP WORK** Ask your classmates about their plans.
Use the time expressions in the box.

A: What are you going to do tonight?
B: I'm going to go to a party.
C: Oh, really? Who's going to be there?
B: Well, Lara and Rosa are going to come.
      But Jeff isn't going to be there....

time expressions	
tonight	next week
tomorrow	next month
tomorrow afternoon	next summer
tomorrow night	next year

10 WORD POWER *Ways to celebrate*

A ▶ Listen and practice.

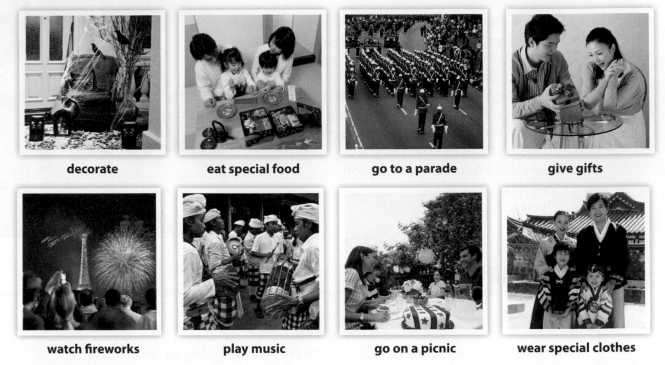

decorate   eat special food   go to a parade   give gifts

watch fireworks   play music   go on a picnic   wear special clothes

B **PAIR WORK** Are you going to celebrate a special day this year? Are you (or is someone you know) going to do any of the things in part A?

A: I'm going to go to a wedding next month. I'm going to wear special clothes.
B: Is it a traditional wedding?

11 HOLIDAYS AND FESTIVALS

A **PAIR WORK** Choose any holiday or festival.
Then ask and answer these questions.

What is the holiday or festival?
When is it?
What are you going to do?
Where are you going to go?
Who's going to be there?
When are you going to go?
How are you going to get there?

A: What is the holiday or festival?
B: It's Cinco de Mayo.
A: When is it?
B: It's on May fifth.
A: What are you going to do?
B: I'm going to go to a parade. . . .

Cinco de Mayo in Mexico

Setsubun in Japan

B **CLASS ACTIVITY** Tell the class about your partner's plans.

What are you going to do on
your birthday?

Scan the article. How old is each person going to be?

Elena Buenaventura
Madrid

"My twenty-first birthday is on Saturday, and I'm going to go out with some friends. To wish me a happy birthday, they're going to pull on my ear 21 times – once for each year. It's an old custom. Some people pull on the ear just once, but my friends are very traditional!"

Ka-mei Shi
Taipei

"Tomorrow is my sixteenth birthday. It's a special birthday, so we're going to have a family ceremony. I'm probably going to get some money in 'lucky' envelopes from my relatives. My mother is going to cook noodles – noodles are for a long life."

Mr. and Mrs. Aoki
Kyoto

"My husband is going to be 60 tomorrow. In Japan, the sixtieth birthday is called *kanreki* – it's the beginning of a new life. The color red represents a new life, so children often give something red as a present. What are our children going to give him? A red hat and vest!"

Philippe Joly
Paris

"I'm going to be 30 next week, so I'm going to invite three very good friends out to dinner. In France, when you have a birthday, you often invite people out. In some countries, I know it's the opposite – people take you out."

A Read the article. Then correct these sentences.

1. To celebrate her birthday, Elena is going to pull on her friends' ears.
2. Ka-mei is going to cook some noodles on her birthday.
3. On his birthday, Mr. Aoki is going to buy something red.
4. Philippe's friends are going to take him out to dinner on his birthday.

B GROUP WORK How do people usually celebrate birthdays in your country? Do you have plans for your next birthday? How about the birthday of a friend or a family member? What are you going to do? Tell your classmates.

Imperatives ▶

Get some rest.	**Don't stay** up late.
Drink lots of juice.	**Don't drink** soda.
Take one pill every evening.	**Don't work** too hard.

Complete these sentences. Use the correct forms of the words in the box.

✓call	stay	not go	not drink
see	take	✓not worry	not eat

1. ....*Call*............ a dentist.
2. ....*Don't worry*........ too much.
3. .... two aspirin.
4. .... to school.

5. .... in bed.
6. .... a doctor.
7. .... coffee.
8. .... any candy.

10 **GOOD ADVICE?**

A Write two pieces of advice for each problem.

My feet hurt.

I have a sore wrist.

I have the flu.

I can't sleep at night.

1. ....
....
2. ....
....
3. ....
....
4. ....
....

B **GROUP WORK** Act out the problems from part A. Your classmates give advice.

A: I feel awful!
B: What's the matter?
A: My feet hurt.
B: I have an idea. Take a hot bath. And don't . . .
C: Here's another idea . . .

11 **INTERCHANGE 12** *Helpful advice*

Give advice for some common problems. Go to Interchange 12 on page 126.

1O Simple Ways to Improve Your Health

What are some ways to improve your health? Don't look at the article.

Believe it or not, you can greatly improve your health in 10 very simple ways.

1 Eat breakfast. Breakfast gives you energy for the morning.

2 Go for a walk. Walking is good exercise, and exercise is necessary for good health.

3 Floss your teeth. Don't just brush them. Flossing keeps your gums healthy.

4 Drink eight glasses of water every day. Water helps your body in many ways.

5 Stretch for five minutes. Stretching is important for your muscles.

6 Get enough calcium. Your bones need it. Dairy foods like yogurt, milk, and cheese have calcium.

7 Do something to challenge your brain. For example, do a crossword puzzle or read a new book.

8 Take a "time-out" — a break of about 20 minutes. Do something different. For example, get up and walk. Or sit down and listen to music.

9 Wear a seat belt. Every year, seat belts save thousands of lives.

10 Protect your skin. Use lots of moisturizer and sunscreen.

Source: *Cooking Light*® Magazine

A Read the article. Then complete the sentences.

1. To get exercise, *go for a walk* .
2. To help your bones, .
3. To help your muscles, .
4. To keep your gums healthy, .
5. To have energy for the morning, .
6. To challenge your brain, .

B GROUP WORK What things in the article do you do regularly? What else do you do for your health? Tell your classmates.

Units 11–12 Progress check

SELF-ASSESSMENT

How well can you do these things? Check (✓) the boxes.

I can	Very well	OK	A little
Ask and answer questions about future plans (Ex. 1, 2)	☐	☐	☐
Use future time expressions (Ex. 2)	☐	☐	☐
Understand conversations about problems (Ex. 3)	☐	☐	☐
Talk about problems (Ex. 4)	☐	☐	☐
Ask how people are and give advice (Ex. 4)	☐	☐	☐

1 HOLIDAY SURVEY

A Complete the questions with names of different holidays.

Are you going to . . . ?	Name
eat special food on	....
give gifts on	....
have a party on	....
play music on	....
wear special clothes on	....

B **CLASS ACTIVITY** Are your classmates going to do the things in part A? Go around the class and find out. Try to write a different person's name on each line.

2 PLANS, PLANS, PLANS

Complete these questions with different time expressions.
Then ask a partner the questions.

1. How are you going to get home ....tonight........ ?
2. What time are you going to go to bed .... ?
3. Who's going to be here .... ?
4. Where are you going to go .... ?
5. What are you going to do .... ?
6. Who are you going to eat dinner with .... ?

84

3 LISTENING *What's the matter?*

▶ Listen to six conversations. Number the pictures from 1 to 6.

.... This person needs some ketchup.

.... This person has a backache.

.... This person can't dance very well.

....1.... This person feels sad.

.... This person is going to ride a horse.

.... This person has the flu.

4 THAT'S GREAT ADVICE!

A Write a problem on a piece of paper. Then write advice for the problem on a different piece of paper.

> My ankle hurts.

> Get some muscle cream.

B CLASS ACTIVITY Put the papers with problems and the papers with advice in two different boxes. Then take a new paper from each box. Go around the class and find the right advice for your problem.

A: I feel terrible.
B: What's the matter?
A: My ankle hurts.
B: I can help. Get some eyedrops.
A: That's terrible advice!

A: I feel awful.
C: Why? What's wrong?
A: My ankle hurts.
C: I know! Get some muscle cream.
A: That's great advice. Thanks!

WHAT'S NEXT?

Look at your Self-assessment again. Do you need to review anything?

13 You can't miss it.

1 WORD POWER Places and things

A ▶ Where can you get these things? Match the things with the places. Then listen and practice. *"You can buy aspirin at a drugstore."*

1. aspirin ....b....
2. bread ....
3. a dictionary ....
4. gasoline ....
5. a sandwich ....
6. stamps ....
7. a suit ....
8. traveler's checks ....

a. a post office

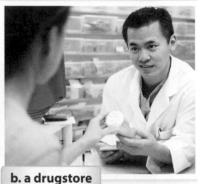

b. a drugstore

c. a gas station

d. a department store

e. a bank

f. a bookstore

g. a coffee shop

h. a supermarket

B PAIR WORK What else can you get or do in the places in part A?

A: You can get a magazine at a bookstore.
B: And you can send a package at the post office.

2 LISTENING *I need a new swimsuit.*

A ⏵ Listen to the Anderson family's conversations. What do they need? Where are they going to get the things? Complete the chart.

	What	Where
1. Jean	a swimsuit	....
2. Mom	....	....
3. Dad	....	....
4. Mike	....	....

B **PAIR WORK** What do you need? Where are you going to get it? Tell your partner.

"I need a snack, so I'm going to go to a coffee shop. . . ."

3 CONVERSATION *It's an emergency!*

⏵ Listen and practice.

    Man: Excuse me. Can you help me? Is there a public restroom around here?

Woman: A public restroom? Hmm. I'm sorry. I don't think so.

    Man: Oh, no. My son needs a restroom – now. It's an emergency!

Woman: Oh, dear. Well, there's a restroom in the department store on Main Street.

    Man: Where on Main Street?

Woman: It's on the corner of Main and First Avenue.

    Man: On the corner of Main and First?

Woman: Yes, it's across from the park. You can't miss it.

    Man: Thanks a lot.

4 PRONUNCIATION *Compound nouns*

A ⏵ Listen and practice. Notice the stress in these compound nouns.

●	●	●	●
post office	gas station	restroom	coffee shop
●	●	●	●
drugstore	bookstore	supermarket	department store

B **PAIR WORK** Practice these sentences. Pay attention to the stress in the compound nouns.

There's a restroom in the drugstore.
There's a bookstore in the department store.

There isn't a post office in the supermarket.
There isn't a coffee shop in the gas station.

Prepositions of place ▶

| on | on the corner of | across from | next to | between |

The department store is **on** Main Street.
It's **on the corner of** Main and First.
It's **across from** the park.

It's **next to** the bank.
The bank is **between** the department store **and** the restaurant.

A Look at the map and complete the sentences. Then compare with a partner.

1. The coffee shop is .....*on*..... Second Avenue. It's .... the shoe store.
2. The movie theater is .... Park and Main. It's .... the park.
3. The gas station is .... the parking lot. It's .... First and Center.
4. The post office is .... Center and Second. It's .... the hospital.
5. The bank is .... the restaurant and the department store. It's .... Main Street.

B **PAIR WORK** Where are these places on the map? Ask and answer questions.

the park   the drugstore   the bookstore   the hospital   the shoe store

A: Where is the park?
B: It's between Park and First, across from the department store.

6 LISTENING *Where is it?*

▶ Look at the map in Exercise 5. Listen to four conversations. Where are the people going?

1. .... 2. .... 3. .... 4. ....

7 SNAPSHOT

▶ Listen and practice.

Top Tourist Attractions: New York City

Grand Central Terminal

Times Square

Central Park

The Empire State Building

Rockefeller Center

The Statue of Liberty

Source: www.iloveny.com

What do you know about these places? What makes them popular?
What are some popular tourist attractions in your country?

8 CONVERSATION *Is it far from here?*

▶ Listen and practice.

Tourist: Excuse me, ma'am. Can you help me? How do I get to St. Patrick's Cathedral?

Woman: Just walk up Fifth Avenue to 50th Street. St. Patrick's is on the right.

Tourist: Is it near Rockefeller Center?

Woman: Yes, it's right across from Rockefeller Center.

Tourist: Thank you. And where is the Empire State Building? Is it far from here?

Woman: It's right behind you. Just turn around and look up!

> **Directions** ▶
>
> | | |
> |---|---|
> | **How do I get to** Rockefeller Center? | **How can I get to** Bryant Park? |
> | **Walk up/Go up** Fifth Avenue. | **Walk down/Go down** Fifth Avenue. |
> | **Turn left on** 49th Street. | **Turn right on** 42nd Street. |
> | It's **on the right**. | It's **on the left**. |

A **PAIR WORK** Imagine you are tourists at Grand Central Terminal.
Ask for directions. Follow the arrows.

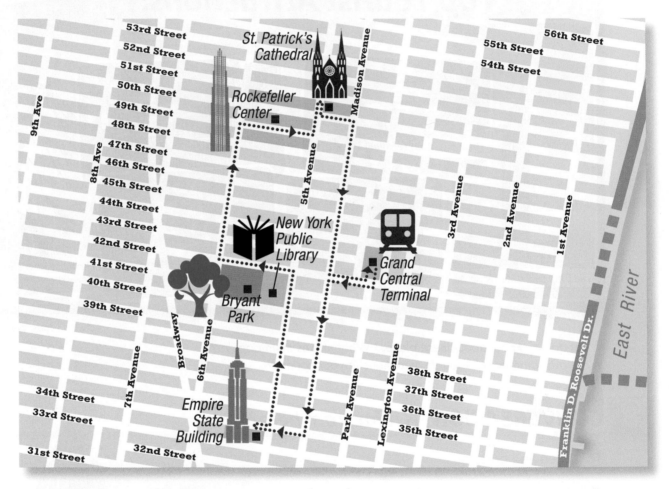

A: Excuse me. How do I get to the Empire State Building?
B: Walk up 42nd Street. Turn left on . . .

B **PAIR WORK** Ask for directions to places near your school.

A: How do I get to the train station?
B: Walk . . .

10 **INTERCHANGE 13** *Giving directions*

Student A, go to Interchange 13A on page 127; Student B, go to Interchange 13B on page 128.

·····Edinburgh's Royal Mile·····

As you read, follow the route on the map below.

1. Start your walking tour at **Edinburgh Castle**. Climb up 187 steps to the top of Castle Hill for a great view. Then take a tour of the castle.

2. Walk down the Royal Mile three blocks to **St. Giles Cathedral**. Go inside and look at the colorful windows.

3. Take a break at **Spoon Café**. Go down the Royal Mile and turn right on South Bridge. The restaurant is on the left.

4. You're almost at the **Museum of Childhood**, on the right on the Royal Mile. There's a great collection of toys, dolls, and games here.

5. Continue down the Royal Mile. Stop at the **Museum of Edinburgh** to learn about the history of Scotland's capital.

6. End your walking tour in **Holyrood Park**, right behind the museum.

A Read the tourist information. Where can you . . . ?

1. rest and eat lunch ....
2. learn about Edinburgh's history ....
3. take a tour ....
4. see beautiful windows ....
5. see old games ....

B **PAIR WORK** Think of places in your city or town. Plan a walking tour of your town.

14 Did you have fun?

1 SNAPSHOT

▶ Listen and practice.

Top Eight Things People Hate to Do

1 stand in line
2 do laundry
3 travel to work
4 go to meetings
5 exercise
6 work in the yard
7 clean the house
8 open the mail

Source: Based on information from *The Book of Lists*

Do you hate to do these things?
What other things do you hate to do? Why?

2 CONVERSATION *I didn't study!*

▶ Listen and practice.

Jason: Hi, Amy. Did you have a good weekend?

Amy: Well, I had a busy weekend, so I'm a little tired today.

Jason: Really? Why?

Amy: Well, on Saturday, I exercised in the morning. Then my roommate and I cleaned, did laundry, and shopped. And then I visited my parents.

Jason: So what did you do on Sunday?

Amy: I studied for the test all day.

Jason: Oh, no! Do we have a test today? I didn't study! I just watched TV all weekend!

GRAMMAR FOCUS

Simple past statements: regular verbs ▶

							Spelling	
I	**studied**	on Sunday.	I	**didn't study**	on Saturday.	stay	→	stay**ed**
You	**watched**	TV.	You	**didn't watch**	a movie.	watch	→	watch**ed**
She	**stayed**	home.	She	**didn't stay**	out.	exercise	→	exercise**d**
We	**shopped**	for groceries.	We	**didn't shop**	for clothes.	study	→	stud**ied**
They	**exercised**	on Saturday.	They	**didn't exercise**	on Sunday.	shop	→	shop**ped**
				did**n't** = did not				

A Tim is talking about his weekend. Complete the sentences.
Then compare with a partner.

On Friday night, I ....*waited*.... (wait) for a phone call,
but my girlfriend ...*didn't call*... (not call). I just
.... (stay) home and .... (watch) TV.
On Saturday, I .... (visit) my friend Frank.
We .... (talk) and .... (listen) to
music. In the evening, he .... (invite) some
friends over, and we .... (cook) a great meal.
I .... (not work) very hard on Sunday. I
.... (not study) at all. I just .... (walk)
to the mall and .... (shop).

B Complete the sentences. Use your own information.
Then compare with a partner.

1. Yesterday, I .... (watch) TV.
2. Last night, I .... (stay) home.
3. Last week, I .... (clean) the house.
4. Last month, I .... (shop) for clothes.
5. Last year, I .... (visit) a different country.

---

4 PRONUNCIATION *Simple past -ed endings*

A ▶ Listen and practice. Notice the pronunciation of **-ed**.

/t/	/d/	/ɪd/
worked	cleaned	invited
watched	stayed	visited
....	....	....
....	....	....

B ▶ Listen and write these verbs under the correct sounds.

cooked   exercised   listened   needed   shopped   waited

GRAMMAR FOCUS

Simple past statements: irregular verbs ▶

I **did** my homework.
I **didn't do** laundry.

You **got up** at noon.
You **didn't get up** at 10:00.

He **went** to the museum.
He **didn't go** to the library.

We **met** our classmates.
We **didn't meet** our teacher.

You **came** home late.
You **didn't come** home early.

They **had** a picnic.
They **didn't have** a party.

A ▶ Complete the chart. Then listen and check.

Present	Past	Present	Past	Present	Past
buy	bought	....	made	....	saw
....	ate	....	read /rɛd/	....	sat
....	felt	....	rode	....	took

B **PAIR WORK** Did you do the things in the pictures yesterday? Tell your partner.

"Yesterday, I did my homework. And I did laundry. . . ."

6

LAST WEEKEND

A Write five things you did and five things you didn't do last weekend.

B **GROUP WORK** Tell your classmates about your weekend.

A: I saw a movie last weekend.
B: I didn't see a movie. But I watched TV.
C: I watched TV, too! I saw . . .

Things I did	Things I didn't do
I saw a movie.	I didn't exercise.
I studied.	I didn't buy clothes.
I . . .	I didn't . . .

CONVERSATION *Did you like it?*

Listen and practice.

Laura: So, did you go anywhere last summer, Erica?
Erica: Yes, I did. My sister and I went to Arizona. We saw the Grand Canyon.
Laura: Really? Did you like it?
Erica: Oh, yes. We loved it!
Laura: Did you go hiking?
Erica: No, we didn't. Actually, we rode horses. And one day we went white-water rafting on the Colorado River!
Laura: Wow! Did you have fun?
Erica: Yes, I did. But my sister didn't like the rafting very much.

8 **GRAMMAR FOCUS**

> ### Simple past yes/no questions
>
> **Did** you **have** a good summer?
>   Yes, I **did**. I **had** a great summer.
> **Did** you **ride** a bicycle?
>   No, I **didn't**. I **rode** a horse.
>
> **Did** Erica **like** her vacation?
>   Yes, she **did**. She **liked** it a lot.
> **Did** Erica and her sister **go** to Colorado?
>   No, they **didn't**. They **went** to Arizona.

A Complete the conversations. Then practice with a partner.

1. A: ......*Did*...... you ......*have*...... (have) a good summer?
   B: Yes, I .... I .... (have) a great summer.
      I .... (go) to the beach a lot.

2. A: .... you .... (go) anywhere last summer?
   B: No, I .... I .... (stay) here. I .... (get) a part-time job, so I .... (make) some extra money.

3. A: .... you .... (take) any classes last summer?
   B: Yes, I .... I .... (take) tennis lessons, and I .... (play) tennis every day!

4. A: .... you .... (speak) English last summer?
   B: No, I .... But I .... (read) English books and I .... (watch) English movies.

B **PAIR WORK** Ask the questions from part A. Answer with your own information.

A: Did you have a good summer?
B: Yes, I did. I went swimming every day.

9 LISTENING *I didn't go anywhere.*

Listen to Andy, Gail, Patrick, and Fran. What did they do last summer? Check (✓) the correct answers.

1. Andy — ☐ stayed home — ☐ visited his brother — ☐ went to the beach
2. Gail — ☐ saw movies — ☐ read books — ☐ watched TV
3. Patrick — ☐ went bike riding — ☐ went swimming — ☐ played tennis
4. Fran — ☐ worked in the yard — ☐ got a job — ☐ painted the house

10 WORD POWER *Summer activities*

A Find two words from the list that go with each verb in the chart. Then listen and check.

camping	old friends	
a class	a picnic	
fun	softball	
✓ a job	swimming	
✓ a new bike	a trip	
new people	volleyball	

get	a job	a new bike
go		
have		
meet		
play		
take		

B **PAIR WORK** Check (✓) six things to ask your partner. Then ask and answer questions.

Did you . . . last summer?

☐ play any sports
☐ buy anything interesting
☐ eat any new foods
☐ meet any interesting people
☐ go anywhere interesting
☐ get a job
☐ play any games
☐ read any books
☐ see any movies
☐ take any trips
☐ take any classes
☐ have fun

A: Did you play any sports last summer?
B: Yes, I did. My friends and I played basketball a lot. We . . .

C **CLASS ACTIVITY** Tell the class about your partner's summer.

"Last summer, Maria went camping with her friend Lucia. They had a lot of fun."

11 INTERCHANGE 14 *Past and present*

Are you different now from when you were a child? Go to Interchange 14 on page 129.

Did you have a good weekend?

Scan the chat room posts. Who had a terrible weekend? Who enjoyed the weekend? Who learned a lot? Who had a busy weekend?

Karen 12:45

I had a great weekend. I went to my best friend Mariela's wedding. She got married in her parents' garden. She wore a fantastic dress! Her parents served a nice meal after the ceremony. I'm really happy for her. And her new husband is really nice!

Pete 1:19

I didn't go outside all weekend. I had so much work to do! On Saturday, I studied all day. On Sunday, I did the dishes, cleaned my apartment, and did laundry. Sunday night, I watched a DVD for my history class. My weekend wasn't relaxing at all!

Lacey 2:02

I had an interesting weekend. I went camping for the first time. My friends and I drove to the campsite on Saturday. First, we put up the tent. Then we built a fire, cooked dinner, and told stories. On Sunday, we went fishing. I didn't really like camping, but I learned a lot.

Jonathan 4:57

I went to a rock concert with some friends. I had an awful time! It took three hours to drive there. I didn't like the band at all. Then on our way home, the car broke down! My parents came and got us. I finally got home at six in the morning. I'm so tired!

A Read the chat room posts. Then correct these sentences.

1. Karen got married. _Karen's best friend got married._
2. After the wedding, everyone went out to eat. ....
3. Pete studied all day on Sunday. ....
4. He watched TV Sunday night. ....
5. Lacey went camping for the third time. ....
6. Lacey liked camping a lot. ....
7. Jonathan went to a rock concert with his parents. ....
8. It took three hours to get home after the concert. ....

B GROUP WORK Do you have a story about an interesting weekend?
Write four sentences about it. Then tell your classmates.

Units 13–14 Progress check

SELF-ASSESSMENT

How well can you do these things? Check (✓) the boxes.

I can	Very well	OK	A little
Understand conversations about where to get things in a town (Ex. 1)	☐	☐	☐
Ask and answer questions about where places are (Ex. 2)	☐	☐	☐
Ask for and give directions (Ex. 2)	☐	☐	☐
Talk about past activities (Ex. 3, 4)	☐	☐	☐
Ask and answer questions about past activities (Ex. 4)	☐	☐	☐

1 LISTENING *What are you looking for?*

▶ Listen to the conversations. What do the people need?
Where can they get or find it? Complete the chart.

What	Where
1.	....
2.	....
3.	....
4.	....

2 WHERE IS THE . . . ?

A **PAIR WORK** Are these places near your school? Where are they?
Ask and answer questions.

bank	coffee shop	hospital	post office
bookstore	department store	park	supermarket

A: Where is the bank?
B: It's on Second Avenue. It's across from the Korean restaurant.

B **PAIR WORK** Give directions from your school to the places in part A.
Your partner guesses the place.

A: Go out of the school and turn left. Walk for about three minutes. It's on
   the right, next to the drugstore.
B: It's the coffee shop.
A: That's right!

3 MY LAST VACATION

A Write four statements about your last vacation.
Two are true and two are false.

> I ate at an expensive restaurant.
> It rained all day, every day.
> I didn't go to a museum.
> I read two books.

B **PAIR WORK** Read your statements. Your partner says
"True" or "False." Who has more correct guesses?

A: On my last vacation, I ate at an expensive restaurant.
B: False.
A: That's right. It's false. OR Sorry. It's true.

4 LAST WEEKEND

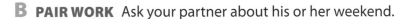

A Check (✓) the things you did last weekend.
Then add two more things you did.

☐ uploaded photos	☐ ate in a restaurant
☐ rode my bicycle	☐ did laundry
☐ cleaned the house	☐ went dancing
☐ played sports	☐ played video games
☐ went shopping	☐ talked on the phone
☐ went to a supermarket	☐ saw a movie
☐ met friends	☐ ....
☐ studied	☐ ....

B **PAIR WORK** Ask your partner about his or her weekend.

A: Did you upload photos last weekend, Keiko?
B: Yes, I did. I uploaded photos of my friends.
   Did you upload photos?
A: No, I didn't. . . .

C **GROUP WORK** Join another pair. Tell them about
your partner's weekend.

"Keiko uploaded photos of her friends."

WHAT'S NEXT?

Look at your Self-assessment again. Do you need to review anything?

15 Where did you grow up?

1 SNAPSHOT

▶ Listen and practice.

Where Were These People Born?

1._____ 2._____ 3._____ 4._____ 5._____

a. the U.S.
b. Colombia
c. France
d. the U.K.
e. Japan

Takashi Murakami, artist | Shakira, singer | Christian Bale, actor | Marion Cotillard, actress | Jon Stewart, TV host

Answers: 1.e 2.b 3.d 4.c 5.a

Source: www.biography.com

Match the people with the countries. Then check your answers at the bottom of the Snapshot. What famous people were born in your country? What do they do?

2 CONVERSATION *I was born in South Korea.*

▶ Listen and practice.

Chuck: Where were you born, Melissa?
Melissa: I was born in South Korea.
Chuck: Oh! So you weren't born in the U.S.
Melissa: No, I came here in 2005.
Chuck: Hmm. You were pretty young.
Melissa: Yeah, I was only seventeen.
Chuck: Did you go to college right away?
Melissa: No, my English wasn't very good, so I took English classes for two years first.
Chuck: Well, your English is really good now.
Melissa: Thanks. Your English is pretty good, too.
Chuck: I hope so! I was born here.

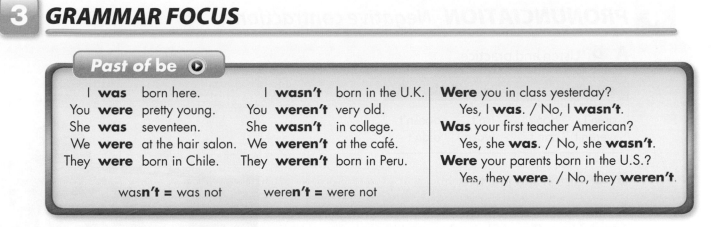

Past of be ▶

I **was** born here.	I **wasn't** born in the U.K.	**Were** you in class yesterday?
You **were** pretty young.	You **weren't** very old.	Yes, I **was**. / No, I **wasn't**.
She **was** seventeen.	She **wasn't** in college.	**Was** your first teacher American?
We **were** at the hair salon.	We **weren't** at the café.	Yes, she **was**. / No, she **wasn't**.
They **were** born in Chile.	They **weren't** born in Peru.	**Were** your parents born in the U.S.?
		Yes, they **were**. / No, they **weren't**.

wasn't = was not   weren't = were not

A Melissa is talking about her family. Choose the correct verb forms. Then compare with a partner.

My family and I ......_were_...... (was / were) all born in South Korea – we .... (wasn't / weren't) born in the U.S. I .... (was / were) born in the city of Incheon, and my brother .... (was / were) born there, too. My parents .... (wasn't / weren't) born in Incheon. They .... (was / were) born in the capital, Seoul. In South Korea, my father .... (was / were) a businessman and my mother .... (was / were) a teacher.

B **PAIR WORK** Look at the picture below. Ask and answer these questions.

1. Was Adam on time for class yesterday?
2. Was it English class?
3. Was it a sunny day?
4. Was it 10:00?

5. Was Mrs. Carter very angry?
6. Were Cindy and Mark late to class?
7. Were they at the board?
8. Were the windows open?

A: Was Adam on time for class yesterday?
B: No, he wasn't. He was late. Was it English class?

4 PRONUNCIATION Negative contractions

A ⊙ Listen and practice.

one syllable		two syllables	
aren't	don't	isn't	doesn't
weren't	can't	wasn't	didn't

B ⊙ Listen and practice.

He **didn't** eat dinner because he **wasn't** hungry.
I **don't** like coffee, and she **doesn't** like tea.
This **isn't** my swimsuit. I **can't** swim.
They **weren't** here yesterday, and they **aren't** here today.

C Write four sentences with negative contractions.
Then read them to a partner.

> I didn't go because my friends weren't there.

5 CONVERSATION I grew up in Texas.

⊙ Listen and practice.

Melissa: So, Chuck, where did you grow up?
Chuck: I grew up in Texas.
Melissa: Were you born there?
Chuck: Yeah. I was born in Dallas.
Melissa: And when did you come to
Los Angeles?
Chuck: In 2000.
Melissa: How old were you then?
Chuck: I was eighteen. I went to
college here.
Melissa: Oh. What was your major?
Chuck: Drama. I was an actor for
five years after college.
Melissa: Really? Why did you become
a hairstylist?
Chuck: Because I needed the money.
And I love it. So, what do you think?
Melissa: Well, uh . . .

6 GRAMMAR FOCUS

> ### Wh-questions with did, was, and were ▶
>
> Where **did** you **grow up**?   I **grew up** in Texas.
> What **did** your father **do** there?   He **worked** in a bank.
> When **did** you **come** to Los Angeles?   I **came** to Los Angeles in 2000.
> Why **did** you **become** a hairstylist?   Because I **needed** the money.
>
> Where **were** you **born**?   I **was born** in Dallas.
> When **were** you **born**?   I **was born** in 1982.
> How old **were** you in 2000?   I **was** eighteen.
> What **was** your major in college?   Drama. I **was** an actor for five years.

A Match the questions with the answers. Then compare with a partner.

1. Where were you born? ....*e*.....   a. Her name was Yumiko.
2. Where did you grow up? ....   b. She was really friendly.
3. How was your first day of school? ....   c. I wanted to improve my English.
4. Who was your first friend in school? ....   d. I grew up in Tokyo.
5. What was he/she like? ....   e. In Hiroshima, Japan.
6. Why did you take this class? ....   f. It was a little scary.

B **PAIR WORK** Ask and answer the questions in part A.
Use your own information.

C **GROUP WORK** Ask the questions. Use a year in
your answers.

1. When were you born?
2. When was your father born?
3. When was your mother born?
4. When did you turn 13?
5. When did you start high school?
6. When did you begin to study English?

saying years
1906 = nineteen oh six
1986 = nineteen eighty-six
2000 = two thousand
2001 = two thousand (and) one
2010 = two thousand (and) ten
OR twenty-ten

7 LISTENING *When was she born?*

A ▶ Listen. When were these people born?
Complete the first column of the chart.

	When were you born?	Where did you grow up?
1. Jill	....	....
2. Roger	....	....
3. Bianca	....	....
4. Ahmed	....	....

B ▶ Listen again. Where did these people grow up?
Complete the second column of the chart.

8 WORD POWER

A ▶ Complete the word map with words from the list. Then listen and check.

✓ cafeteria
classroom
college
computer lab
elementary school
high school
history
junior high school
library
math
physical education
science

Classes
....
....
....
....

Schools
....
....
....
....

School days

Places
cafeteria ....
....
....
....

B **PAIR WORK** Find out about your partner's elementary, junior high, or high school days. Ask these questions. Then tell the class.

What classes did you take?
What was your favorite class? Why?
What classes didn't you like? Why not?
Who was your best friend?

Who was your favorite teacher? Why?
Where did you spend your free time? Why?
What was a typical day of school like?
What didn't you like about school?

"In elementary school, Dan spent his free time in the library because he liked to read. . . ."

9 WHAT DO YOU REMEMBER?

A **GROUP WORK** How often does this English class meet? What do you remember from your last class? Ask and answer these questions.

1. Who was in class? Who wasn't there?
2. Were you early, late, or on time?
3. Where did you sit?
4. What did you talk about?
5. What did you learn about your classmates?
6. What words did you learn?
7. Did you have any homework?
8. What did you do after class?

B **CLASS ACTIVITY** What does your group remember? Tell the class.

10 INTERCHANGE 15 *Life events*

Make a time line of your life. Go to Interchange 15 on page 130.

Turning Pain to Gain

Scan the article. Why does Mackenzie read all the time?

Seven years ago, Mackenzie Bearup hurt her knee. She was just ten years old. A week later, the pain was still there. The pain didn't stop. Then she found out about a disease called RSD. This disease tells the brain her knee is still injured, even though it isn't. There is no cure for the pain. Her knee feels terrible all the time.

Sometimes, Mackenzie felt so awful that she stayed in bed for months. It was very difficult to walk. Her doctors tried everything: medicine, exercise, and other treatments. Nothing worked . . . except books.

Mackenzie read lots of books. The books helped her stop thinking about the pain. And she decided to help other children forget their pain, too.

She found out about a treatment center for children nearby. The center had a new library, but no books. She asked all her friends and her parents' friends to give books. Then she put ads in newspapers and made a website.

Mackenzie's goal was to give 300 books to the library. But she soon had 3,000 books, and more were on the way! Today, that number is more than 40,000. She started an organization. Sheltering Books now helps children in many states in the U.S.

Mackenzie's knee still hurts all the time. But she feels better because she's helping other kids with their pain.

A Read the article. Then write a question for each answer.

1. When did Mackenzie hurt her knee .... ?   Seven years ago.
2. .... ?   She felt terrible.
3. .... ?   Medicine, exercise, and other treatments.
4. .... ?   They helped her forget her pain.
5. .... ?   She asked her family and friends.
6. .... ?   To give 300 books.

B Number these events in Mackenzie's life from 1 (first) to 7 (last).

.... a. She made a website.
.... b. She found out about RSD.
...1... c. She hurt her knee.
.... d. She started an organization.

.... e. She discovered books helped her pain.
.... f. She asked her friends for books.
.... g. She tried lots of different treatments.

C **GROUP WORK** Why do you think books help people with pain?
Can you think of other things that could help? Tell your classmates.

16 Can she call you later?

1 CONVERSATION *She's in a meeting.*

▶ Listen and practice.

Receptionist: Good morning. Digital Media.
Tony: Hello. Can I speak to Kathy Wilson, please?
Receptionist: I'm sorry, but she's in a meeting right now.
Tony: Oh.
Receptionist: Can I take a message?
Tony: Yes, thanks. This is her friend Tony.
Please ask her to call me at home.
Receptionist: Does she have your number?
Tony: Yes, she does.
Receptionist: OK. I'll give her your message.
Tony: Thank you so much.

2 WORD POWER *Prepositional phrases*

A ▶ Listen and practice.

at home	**at** the mall	**in** bed	**in** the shower	**on** vacation
at work	**at** the library	**in** class	**in** the hospital	**on** a trip
at school	**at** the beach	**in** Mexico	**in** a meeting	**on** his/her break

at work

in a meeting

on her break

B PAIR WORK Make a list of five friends and family members.
Give it to your partner. Where are these people right now?
Ask and answer questions.

A: Where's your brother right now?
B: He's on vacation. He's in Thailand.

3 LISTENING *I was in the shower.*

A 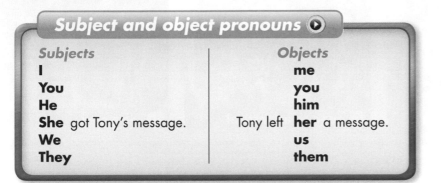 Listen to Brian return three phone calls. Where was he? Complete the sentences.

1. He was ......*in the shower*...... .
2. He was ....
3. He was ....

B ▶ Listen again. What did the callers ask? Correct the questions.

1. Donna: "Can you please call?"
2. Jun: "Can I see your notes from class today?"
3. Ruth: "Can you study on Saturday night?"

4 GRAMMAR FOCUS

Subject and object pronouns ▶

Subjects		Objects	
I		**me**	
You		**you**	
He		**him**	
She	got Tony's message.	Tony left **her**	a message.
We		**us**	
They		**them**	

A Complete the phone conversations with the correct pronouns. Then practice with a partner.

1. A: Can ......*I*......... speak with Ms. Fee, please?
   B: .... 's not here. But maybe .... can help you.
   A: Please give .... my new phone number. It's 555-2981.

2. A: Hi, this is David. Is Mr. Roberts there?
   B: .... 'm sorry, but .... 's not here right now. Do you want to leave a message?
   A: Yes. Please tell .... to call me at work.

3. A: Hello, this is Carol's Café. Are Kate and Joe in?
   B: No, ... 're not. Can .... help you?
   A: .... found Kate and Joe's keys. .... left .... on the table.
   B: Just bring .... the keys. I can give .... to Kate and Joe.
   A: I'm sorry, but .... can't. Can Kate and Joe call .... ?
   B: OK.

B **PAIR WORK** Roleplay this phone conversation.

Student A: "Call" your friend Calvin. He needs your new phone number.
Student B: Answer the phone. Calvin is not in. Take a message.

C **PAIR WORK** Change roles. This time give an email address.

5 SNAPSHOT

▶ Listen and practice.

Popular Activities in the U.S.

○ go to the movies

○ go to a concert

○ go to an amusement park

○ see a sports event

○ go to an art festival

○ see a play

Source: The U.S. Census Bureau

Check (✓) the activities that are popular in your country.
What other activities are popular in your country?
What are your favorite activities? Why?

6 CONVERSATION *I'd love to!*

▶ Listen and practice.

Tony: Hello?

Kathy: Hi, Tony. It's Kathy. I got your message.

Tony: Hi. Thanks for calling me back. Sorry I called you at work.

Kathy: Oh, that's OK. But I have to get back soon. What's up?

Tony: Well, do you want to see a movie with me tonight?

Kathy: Tonight? I'm sorry, but I can't. I have to work late tonight.

Tony: Oh, that's too bad. How about tomorrow night?

Kathy: Uh, . . . sure. I'd love to. What time do you want to meet?

Tony: How about around seven o'clock?

Kathy: Terrific!

7 PRONUNCIATION *Reduction of* want to *and* have to

A ▶ Listen and practice. Notice the reduction of **want to** and **have to**.

        /wanə/
A: Do you **want to** go to a party with me tonight?
              /hæftə/
B: I'm sorry, but I can't. I **have to** study for a test.

B **PAIR WORK** Practice the conversation in Exercise 6 again. Try to reduce **want to** and **have to**.

go to a party

8 GRAMMAR FOCUS

Invitations; verb + to ▶

Do you want to see a movie with me tonight?	**Would you like to go** to an art festival?
Sure. I**'d** really **like to** see a good comedy.	Yes, I**'d love to** (go to an art festival)!
I**'d like to** (see a movie), but I **have to** work late.	I**'d like to** (go), but I **need to** study.

I**'d** = I would

A Complete the invitations. Then match them with the responses.

Invitations

1. Would you ......*like to*...... go to an
   amusement park this weekend? .....*d*.....
2. Do you .... go to a basketball
   game tomorrow night? ....
3. Would you .... see a play
   tonight? ....
4. Do you .... go swimming on
   Saturday? ....
5. Do you .... play soccer after
   school today? ....
6. Would you .... go to a hip-hop
   concert on Saturday night? ....

Responses

a. I'd like to, but I don't have
   a swimsuit!
b. I'm sorry, but I have to talk to
   the teacher after school.
c. I don't really like basketball. Do you want
   to do something else?
d. I'd like to, but I can't. I'm going to go
   on a trip this weekend.
e. Yes, I'd love to. It's my favorite type
   of music.
f. Tonight? I can't. I need to help
   my parents.

B **PAIR WORK** Practice the invitations from part A.
Respond with your own information.

A: Would you like to go to an amusement park this weekend?
B: I'd like to, but I can't. I have to . . .

9 EXCUSES, EXCUSES!

A Do you ever use these excuses? Check (✓) Often, Sometimes, or Never. Compare with a partner.

	Often	Sometimes	Never
I have to babysit.	☐	☐	☐
I need to study for a test.	☐	☐	☐
I have to work late.	☐	☐	☐
I need to go to bed early.	☐	☐	☐
I want to visit my family.	☐	☐	☐
I have a class.	☐	☐	☐
I have a headache.	☐	☐	☐
I'm not feeling well.	☐	☐	☐
I need to do laundry.	☐	☐	☐
I already have plans.	☐	☐	☐

I have to babysit.

B Write down three things you want to do this weekend.

I want to go to the baseball game on Saturday.

C **CLASS ACTIVITY** Go around the class and invite your classmates to do the things from part B. Your classmates respond with excuses.

A: Would you like to go to the baseball game on Saturday?
B: I'm sorry, but I can't. I need to do laundry on Saturday.

10 LISTENING *I'd love to, but . . .*

A ▶ Tony invited some people to a party. Listen to his voice-mail messages. Who can come? Who can't come? Check (✓) the correct answers.

	Can come	Can't come	Excuse
1. Roy	☐	☐	....
2. Angie	☐	☐	....
3. Brad	☐	☐	....
4. Teresa	☐	☐	....
5. Aaron	☐	☐	....

B ▶ Listen again. Why can't some people come? Write their excuses.

11 INTERCHANGE 16 *Let's make a date!*

Make a date with your classmates. Go to Interchange 16 on page 131.

Around Los Angeles *this weekend* (search)

> **Look at the events. Which would you like to go to? Number the pictures from 1 (very interesting) to 5 (not interesting).**

HOME	**EVENTS**	RESTAURANTS	SHOPPING	HOTELS	CELEBRITIES	DEALS

Friday Saturday Sunday

Festivals:
Bella Via Street Painting Festival
Santa Clarita
All day
Bella Via is Italian for "beautiful street." Watch as artists turn the streets into works of art. This event features food, live music, a 5-kilometer race, and children's activities.

Music:
Concert at Hollywood Bowl
7:00 P.M. to midnight
Come hear some great music under the stars! Six terrific bands are going to get your feet moving. Sandwiches, pizza, and drinks for sale.

Movies:
Los Angeles Film Festival
Various Theaters in Westwood
Check listings for times.
Do you want to see the best North American films of the year? More than 200 films. Seats sell out fast, so get tickets now.

Art:
Fiesta Hermosa Arts and Crafts Fair

Hermosa Beach
Starts at 11:00 A.M.
Do you need to decorate your home? Visit this colorful art fair. Find paintings, crafts, and photographs. Jewelry, too! Food and live music.

Attractions:
Aquarium of the Pacific
Whale Tour
11:30 A.M. and 3:00 P.M.
Do you want to see the largest animal on the planet? Go on a boat  tour and learn about the amazing blue whale. Then visit the aquarium to see thousands of beautiful fish and sea birds.

A Read the web page. Where can you do these things? Write two places.

1. buy clothes or jewelry	....	....
2. buy food	....	....
3. sit indoors	....	....
4. be outdoors	....	....
5. see a live performance	....	....

B GROUP WORK Where do you like to go in your city or town? What events do you like? Tell your classmates.

Units 15–16 Progress check

SELF-ASSESSMENT

How well can you do these things? Check (✓) the boxes.

I can	Very well	OK	A little
Talk about my past (Ex. 1)	☐	☐	☐
Ask about famous people using simple past yes/no questions (Ex. 2)	☐	☐	☐
Ask and answer questions about someone's past (Ex. 2)	☐	☐	☐
Understand phone calls and leave or pass on messages (Ex. 3)	☐	☐	☐
Ask and answer questions about things I want, need, and have to do (Ex. 4)	☐	☐	☐
Make and respond to invitations (Ex. 5)	☐	☐	☐

1 INTERVIEW

A **PAIR WORK** Choose three years in your partner's life. Then ask your partner the questions and complete the chart.

	19___	20___	20___
How old were you in . . . ?	....	....	....
Where were your friends in . . . ?	....	....	....
What were you like in . . . ?	....	....	....

B **CLASS ACTIVITY** Tell the class about your partner's life.

"In 1999, Raul was four. He . . ."

2 WHO WAS HE?

GROUP WORK Think of a famous person from the past. Your classmates ask yes/no questions to guess the person.

Was he/she born in . . . ?
Was he/she a singer? an actor?
Was he/she tall? heavy? good-looking?

A: I'm thinking of a famous man from the past.
B: Was he born in the U.S.?
A: No, he wasn't.
C: Was he . . . ?

3 LISTENING On the phone

Listen and check (✓) the best response.

1. ☐ Yes. Please tell her to call me.
   ☐ Yes. Please tell him to call me.

2. ☐ Sure. Does he have your number?
   ☐ No, sorry. He's not here right now.

3. ☐ Yes, you do.
   ☐ No, I don't.

4. ☐ I'm going to visit my parents.
   ☐ I had a terrible headache.

5. ☐ I'd love to, but I can't.
   ☐ No, I didn't go. I was at work.

6. ☐ I'm sorry. He's not here right now.
   ☐ No, Sandra is at work right now.

4 FIND SOMEONE WHO . . .

A CLASS ACTIVITY Go around the class. Ask questions to complete the chart. Try to write a different name on each line.

Find someone who . . .	Name
needs to do laundry this weekend	....
wants to go home early	....
has to babysit this week	....
wants to go shopping this weekend	....
wants to see a movie tonight	....
has to go to the doctor this week	....
needs to work this weekend	....
doesn't want to do homework tonight	....

A: Megumi, do you need to do laundry this weekend?
B: Yes, I do.

B PAIR WORK Share your answers with a partner.

5 INVITATIONS

A Make a list of five things you want to do this weekend.

B CLASS ACTIVITY Go around the class. Invite your classmates to do the things from part A. Your classmates accept or refuse the invitations.

A: Would you like to go to a museum this weekend?
B: I'm sorry, but I can't. I have to . . .

C: Do you want to go to a soccer match on Sunday?
D: Sure, I'd love to! When would you like to . . . ?

WHAT'S NEXT?

Look at your Self-assessment again. Do you need to review anything?

Interchange activities

FAMOUS CLASSMATES

A Imagine you are a famous person. Write your name, phone number, and email address on the card.

Name: Rafael Nadal
Phone: 646-555-0831
Email: rafaelnadal@cup.org

Name: ....
Phone: ....
Email: ....

B CLASS ACTIVITY Go around the class. Introduce yourself to three "famous people." Ask and answer questions to complete the cards.

A: Hi. My name is Angelina Jolie.
B: I'm Rafael Nadal. Nice to meet you, Angelina.
A: Rafael, what's your email address?
B: It's R-A-F-A-E-L N-A-D-A-L at C-U-P dot O-R-G.
A: I'm sorry. Can you repeat that?

useful expressions
I'm sorry.
Can you repeat that?
How do you spell that?

Name: ....
Phone: ....
Email: ....

Name: ....
Phone: ....
Email: ....

Name: ....
Phone: ....
Email: ....

PAIR WORK How are the two pictures different?
Ask questions to find the differences.

A: Where are the sunglasses?
B: In picture 1, they're next to the television.
A: In picture 2, they're in front of the television.

Picture 1

Picture 2

CELEBRITY FASHIONS

GROUP WORK Take turns. Describe the people at the party.
Don't say the person's name. Your classmates guess the person.

A: He's wearing blue jeans, a yellow shirt, and a black jacket. Who is it?
B: Is it Daniel Radcliffe?
A: No, it isn't.
C: Is it Will Smith?
A: That's right.

B: They're wearing dresses. Who are they?
C: Are they Sandra Bullock and Cameron Diaz?
B: That's right.

Will Smith

Kristen Stewart

Daniel Radcliffe

Penelope Cruz

Sandra Bullock

Cameron Diaz

David Beckham

George Clooney

Robert Pattinson

Jennifer Lopez

Helen Mirren

Prince William

Anne Hathaway

Rain

Jackie Chan

Johnny Depp

A PAIR WORK Play the board game. Follow these instructions.

1. Choose a marker. Place it on **Start**.
2. Student A tosses a coin and moves one or two spaces.

   "Heads" means move two spaces.
   "Tails" means move one space.

heads   tails

3. Student A asks Student B a question with the words in the space.
4. Take turns. Continue until both markers are on **Finish**.

A: It's "heads." I move two spaces. What's your last name?
B: It's Lee. Now it's my turn!

useful expressions
It's your turn.
It's my turn.
I don't know.

START

first name What's your ?

name What's your last ?

you How name last ? do your spell A B C

phone your number ? What's 0 2 5

your What's 中文 language 日本語 ? Español first

like your What's ? hometown

are ? you from Where

best Who's your friend ?

best your ? What's like friend

? your email address What's

What you ? like are

FINISH

B CLASS ACTIVITY Tell the class two things about your partner.

"Ricardo is from Quito. Quito is beautiful and very exciting."

WHAT'S WRONG WITH THIS PICTURE?

GROUP WORK What's wrong with this picture? Tell your classmates.

"Ellen is swimming, but she's wearing high heels and a hat!"

A CLASS ACTIVITY Go around the class and find this information.
Try to write a different name on each line.

Find someone who . . .

	Name		Name
gets up at 5:00 A.M. on weekdays	....	takes a bus to class	....
gets up at noon on Saturdays	....	rides a motorcycle to class	....
does homework on Sunday night	....	cooks on weekends	....
works at night	....	plays the drums	....
works on weekends	....	has two brothers	....
has a pet	....	checks email every day	....
lives in the suburbs	....	speaks three languages	....
lives alone	....	doesn't eat breakfast	....

have a pet

play the drums

speak three languages

Allô?

Hello?

Moshi Moshi!

A: Do you get up at 5:00 A.M. on weekends, Jung-ho?
B: No, I get up at 7:00 A.M.
A: Do you get up at 5:00 A.M. on weekdays, Victor?
C: Yes, I get up at 5:00 A.M. every day.

B GROUP WORK Compare your answers.

A: Victor gets up at 5:00 A.M.
B: Maria gets up at 5:00 A.M., too.
C: Jung-ho gets up at . . .

A **PAIR WORK** Find the differences between Bill's apartment and Rachel's apartment.

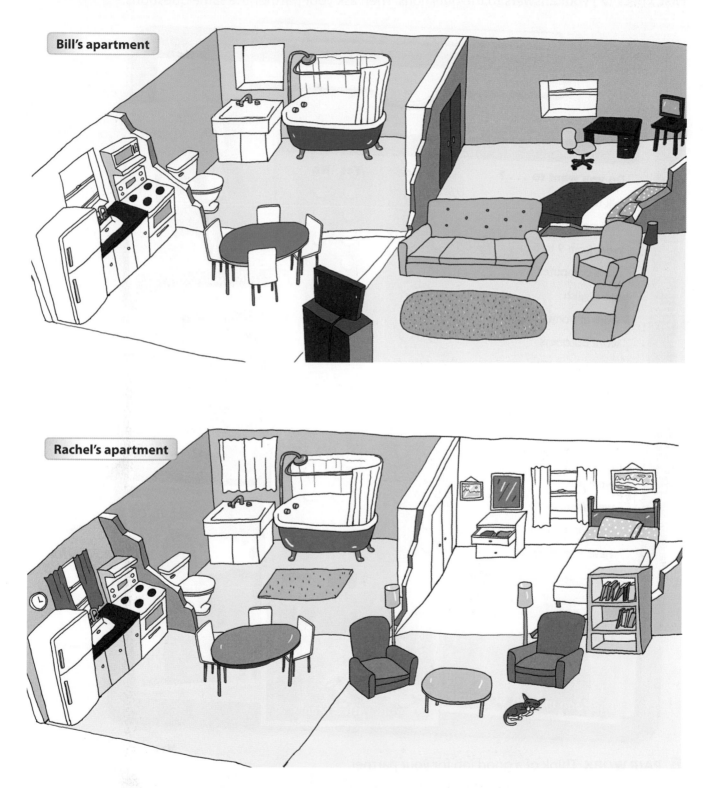

Bill's apartment

Rachel's apartment

A: There are four chairs in Bill's kitchen, but there are three chairs in Rachel's kitchen.
B: There's a sofa in Bill's living room, but there's no sofa in Rachel's living room.

B **GROUP WORK** Compare your answers.

A PAIR WORK Imagine you're looking for a job. What do you want to do?
First, check (✓) your answers to the questions. Then ask your partner the same questions.

Do you want to . . . ?	Me		My partner	
	Yes	No	Yes	No
talk to people	○	○	○	○
help people	○	○	○	○
work from 9 to 5	○	○	○	○
use a computer	○	○	○	○
use English	○	○	○	○
work at home	○	○	○	○
work outdoors	○	○	○	○
work in an office	○	○	○	○
perform in front of people	○	○	○	○
be on TV	○	○	○	○
travel	○	○	○	○
work with a team	○	○	○	○
wear a suit	○	○	○	○
wear blue jeans	○	○	○	○
have an exciting job	○	○	○	○
have a relaxing job	○	○	○	○

work from 9 to 5

work outdoors

be on TV

perform in front of people

work with a team

B PAIR WORK Think of a good job for your partner.

A: You want to use English, travel, and have an exciting job.
 Do you want to be a tour guide?
B: No, a tour guide's job is very stressful.
A: Well, do you want to be . . . ?

SNACK SURVEY

A Complete the snack survey. Use these foods and other foods you know.

beef jerky

grapes

corn chips

watermelon

ice cream

cake

potato chips

candy

popcorn

cookies

pizza

pineapple

hot dogs

peanuts

chocolates

almonds

Snacks I often eat	Snacks I sometimes eat	Snacks I never eat
....	....	....
....	....	....
....	....	....
....	....	....
....	....	....
....	....	....
....	....	....

B **PAIR WORK** Compare your information.

A: I often eat watermelon.
B: I never eat watermelon. I sometimes eat popcorn.

A **CLASS ACTIVITY** Go around the class. Find someone who can and someone who can't do each thing. Try to write a different name on each line.

Names		
Can you . . . ?	**Can**	**Can't**
play two musical instruments	....	....
whistle a song	....	....
say "Hello" in three languages	....	....
swim underwater	....	....
raise one eyebrow	....	....
do a handstand	....	....
fix a computer	....	....
make your own clothes	....	....
say the alphabet backward	....	....
wiggle your ears	....	....

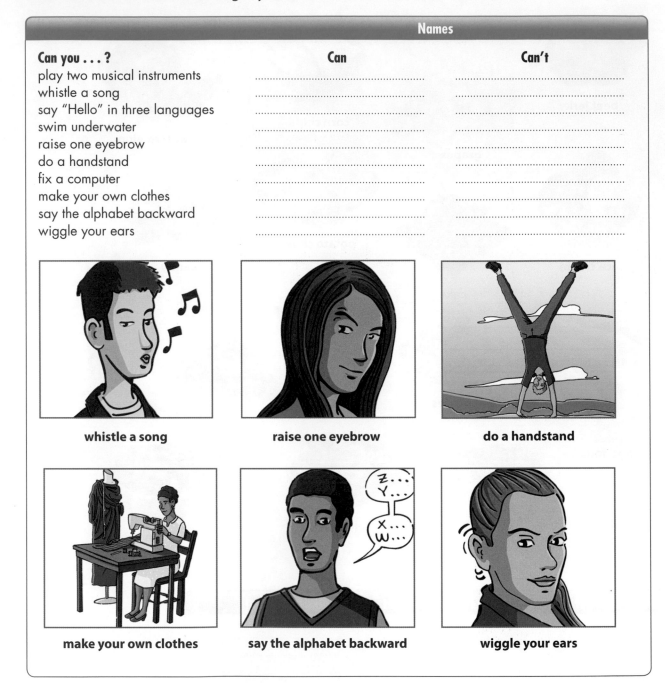

whistle a song   raise one eyebrow   do a handstand

make your own clothes   say the alphabet backward   wiggle your ears

A: Can you play two musical instruments?
B: Yes, I can. OR No, I can't.

B **CLASS ACTIVITY** Share your answers with the class.

"Mei-li can't play two musical instruments, but Claudia can. She can play the violin and the piano."

C Do you have any other "hidden talents"?

A **PAIR WORK** Is your partner going to do any of these things? Check (✓) your guesses.

Is your partner going to . . . ?

	My guesses		My partner's answers	
	Yes	No	Yes	No
1. have a snack after class	☐	☐	☐	☐
2. watch TV tonight	☐	☐	☐	☐
3. go to bed late tomorrow night	☐	☐	☐	☐
4. go out with friends tomorrow night	☐	☐	☐	☐
5. go dancing this weekend	☐	☐	☐	☐
6. eat at a restaurant this weekend	☐	☐	☐	☐
7. go to the gym next week	☐	☐	☐	☐
8. buy something expensive this month	☐	☐	☐	☐
9. go on a trip next month	☐	☐	☐	☐
10. get a job next summer	☐	☐	☐	☐

B **PAIR WORK** Ask and answer questions to check your guesses.

A: Are you going to watch TV tonight?
B: Yes, I am. I'm going to watch my favorite show.

C **CLASS ACTIVITY** How many of your guesses are correct?
Who has the most correct guesses?

Student B

A **PAIR WORK** Look at the map. You are on Third Avenue between
Maple and Oak Streets. Your partner asks you for directions to three places.
(There are signs for these places on your map.) Use the expressions in the
box to give directions.

A: Excuse me. How do I get to the garage?
B: Walk down Third Avenue to . . .

Go up/Go down . . .	It's on the corner of . . . Street	It's next to . . .
Walk up/Walk down . . .	and . . . Avenue.	It's behind . . .
Turn right/Turn left . . .	It's between . . . and . . .	It's in front of . . .
		It's across from . . .

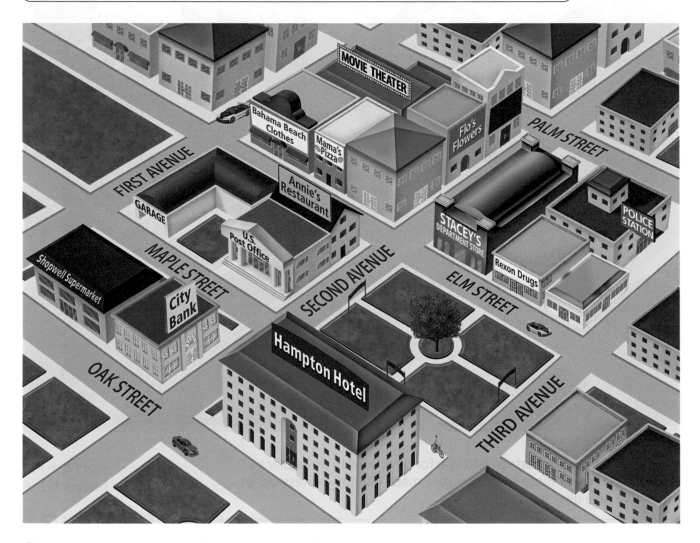

B **PAIR WORK** Ask your partner for directions to these places.
(There are no signs for these places on your map.) Then label the buildings.

coffee shop   shoe store   bookstore

A **PAIR WORK** Ask your partner questions about his or her past and present.
Check (✓) the answers.

A: Did you argue with your friends as a child?
B: Yes, I did. OR No, I didn't.

A: Do you argue with your friends now?
B: Yes, I do. OR No, I don't.

Did you ... as a child?
Do you ... now?

	As a child		Now	
	Yes	No	Yes	No
argue with your friends	☐	☐	☐	☐
clean your room	☐	☐	☐	☐
make your bed	☐	☐	☐	☐
get up early	☐	☐	☐	☐
sleep late on Saturdays	☐	☐	☐	☐
have a computer	☐	☐	☐	☐
listen to rock music	☐	☐	☐	☐
play a musical instrument	☐	☐	☐	☐
play a sport	☐	☐	☐	☐
ride a bicycle	☐	☐	☐	☐
wear glasses	☐	☐	☐	☐
wear braces	☐	☐	☐	☐

play a musical instrument

make your bed

wear braces

argue with your friends

B **GROUP WORK** Join another pair. Tell them about changes in your partner's life.

"Hee-jin argued with her friends as a child, but she doesn't argue with her friends now."

A What were five important events in your life? Mark the years and events on the time line. Then write a sentence about each one.

I was born . . .

I started elementary school . . .

I won an award . . .

I opened a bank account . . .

I traveled with friends . . .

I graduated from high school . . .

I moved to a new place . . .

I started college . . .

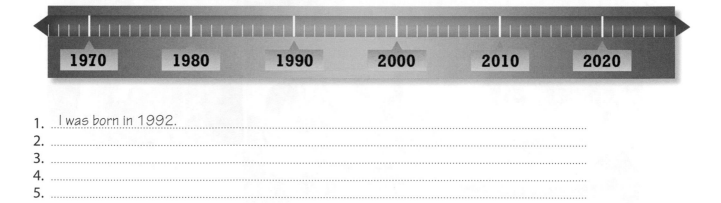

1970   **1980**   **1990**   **2000**   **2010**   **2020**

1. I was born in 1992.
2. ....
3. ....
4. ....
5. ....

B PAIR WORK Ask your partner about his or her time line.

A: What happened in 2003?
B: I moved to a new place.
A: How old were you?
B: I was twelve.

A Imagine this is next month's calendar. Write 10 plans on the calendar. Use these expressions and your own ideas.

go to (the movies/a party)
go (dancing/shopping)
go (on a trip/on vacation)
study for (a test/an exam)
go out with (my girlfriend/boyfriend)

play (basketball/video games)
meet (my friend/teacher)
have dinner with (my brother/parents)
visit (my parents/grandparents)
see (the dentist/doctor)

SUNDAY	MONDAY	TUESDAY	WEDNESDAY	THURSDAY	FRIDAY	SATURDAY
1	2	3	4	5	6	7
8	9	10	11	12	13	14
15	16	17	18	19	20	21
22	23	24	25	26	27	28
29	30	31				

B **GROUP WORK** Look at your calendars. Agree on a date to do something together.

A: Do you want to do something on March third?
B: I'd like to, but I can't. I'm going to play volleyball then. How about March fourth?
C: That works for me. What time?

C **GROUP WORK** Now decide what to do together. Then share your plans with the class.

A: We can all do something on March fourth. Would you like to play video games?
B: No, I don't like to play video games very much. Do you want to go to a museum?
C: Well, I really don't like museums. . . .

Unit 7

1 Simple present short answers (page 45)

▶ Remember: I/You/We/They **do/don't**. He/She/It **does/doesn't**.

Circle the correct words.

A: **Do / Does** your family **live / lives** in an apartment?

B: No, we **don't / doesn't**. We **have / has** a house.

A: That's nice. **Do / Does** your house have two floors?

B: Yes, it **do / does**. It **have / has** four rooms on the first floor. And we **have / has** three bedrooms and a bathroom on the second floor.

A: And **do / does** you and your family **have / has** a yard?

B: Yes, we **do / does**. And how about you, Tim? **Do / Does** you **live / lives** in a house, too?

A: No, I **don't / doesn't**. My wife and I **have / has** a small apartment in the city.

B: Oh. **Do / Does** you **like / likes** the city?

A: Yes, I **do / does**. But my wife **don't / doesn't**.

2 *There is, there are* (page 47)

▶ Use *there is* with singular nouns: **There's** a bed. Use *there are* with plural nouns: **There are** two chairs.

▶ Use *some* in affirmative statements: There are **some** chairs in the kitchen. Use *any* in negative statements: There aren't **any** chairs in the bedroom.

Read the information about the Diaz family's new house. Write sentences with the phrases in the box.

there's a	there are some
there's no	there are no
there isn't a	there aren't any

1.	A living room?	Yes
2.	A dining room?	No
3.	A dishwasher in the kitchen?	No
4.	A table in the kitchen?	Yes
5.	Curtains on the windows?	Yes
6.	Rugs on the floors?	No
7.	Closets in the bedrooms?	Yes
8.	Bookcases in the bedrooms?	No

1. There's a living room.
2. ....
3. ....
4. ....
5. ....
6. ....
7. ....
8. ....

Unit 8

1 Simple present Wh-questions (page 52)

▶ Use *What* to ask about things: **What do** you do? Use *Where* to ask about places: **Where do** you work? Use *How do/does . . . like . . . ?* to ask for an opinion: **How does** he **like** his job?

Complete the conversations.

1. A: What _does your husband do_ ?
   B: My husband? Oh, he's a nurse.
   A: Really? Where .... ?
   B: He works at Mercy Hospital.
2. A: Where .... ?
   B: I work in a restaurant.
   A: Nice! What .... ?
   B: I'm a cook.
3. A: How .... ?
   B: My job? I don't really like it very much.
   A: That's too bad. What .... ?
   B: I'm a manager. I work at a clothing store.
4. A: What .... ?
   B: My brother is a doctor, and my sister is a lawyer.
   A: How .... ?
   B: They work very hard, but they love their jobs.

2 Placement of adjectives (page 54)

▶ Adjectives come after the verb *be*: A doctor's job **is stressful**. Adjectives come before nouns: A police officer has a **dangerous job**. (NOT: ~~A police officer has a job dangerous.~~)
▶ Adjectives have the same form with singular or plural nouns: Firefighters and police officers have stressful jobs. (NOT . . . have ~~stressfuls~~ jobs.)

Use the information to write two sentences.

1. accountant / job / boring
   An accountant's job is boring.
   An accountant has a boring job.

2. salesperson / job / stressful
   ....
   ....

3. security guard / job / dangerous
   ....
   ....

4. nurse / job / exciting
   ....
   ....

5. taxi driver / job / interesting
   ....
   ....

6. electrician / job / difficult
   ....
   ....

Unit 9

1 Count and noncount nouns; *some* and *any*

1. A: What do you want for lunch?
   B: Let's make **some** sandwiches.
   A: Good idea! Do we have **any** bread?
   B: I think there's **some** in the refrigerator. Let me see. . . . No, I don't see **any**.
   A: Well, let's go to the store. We need **some** milk, too. And do we have **any** cheese?
   B: Yes, we do. There's **some** cheese here, and there are **some** tomatoes, too.
   A: Do we have **any** mayonnaise? I love **some** mayonnaise on my sandwiches.
   B: Me, too. But there isn't **any** here. Let's buy **some**.
2. A: Let's make a big breakfast tomorrow morning.
   B: OK. What do we need? Are there **any** eggs?
   A: There are **some**, but I think we need to buy **some** more.
   B: OK. And let's get **some** yogurt, too. We don't have **any**, and I love yogurt for breakfast.
   A: Me, too. Do you see **any** bread in the refrigerator?
   B: Yes there's **some** in the refrigerator.
   A: Great! So we don't need to buy **any** at the store.
   B: That's right. Just eggs and yogurt!

2 Adverbs of frequency

B: I **often** go to a restaurant near work.
A: Do you **ever** eat at your desk?
B: No, I **hardly ever** stay in for lunch.
A: And what do you **usually** have?
B: I **always** have soup and a sandwich.
A: Me, too. I **never** have a big lunch.

Unit 10

1 Simple present Wh-questions

2. **Who do** you go to games with? a
3. **How** often **does** your team play? d
4. **When do** they play? e
5. **Where do** they play? f
6. **What** time **do** the games start? b

2 *Can* for ability

A

2. John can play the piano and the violin.
3. Brad and George can act, but they can't sing.
4. Maria can snowboard, but she can't ice skate.
5. Justin can't upload photos or download a video.
6. Lisa can't write poems but she can tell good jokes.

B

2. Lisa can.   4. Yes, he can.   6. He can act.
3. Yes, she can. 5. Maria can.

Unit 11

1 The future with *be going to*

Tomorrow **is going to be** a very exciting day. It's my birthday, and my friends and I **are going to celebrate**. In the morning, Scott and I **are going to drive** to the beach. Our friend Sara **is going to meet** us there. We**'re going to stay** at the beach for a few hours. Then we**'re going to have** lunch at my favorite restaurant. After lunch, Scott **is going to go** to work, and Sara and I **are going to see** a movie. After the movie, we**'re going to go** to our friend Charlie's house. He **is going to cook** dinner for Sara and me.

2. Q: Are Scott and Robert going to take the bus to the beach?
   A: No, they're going to drive to the beach.
4. Q: Are the friends going to have lunch at a restaurant?
   A: Yes, they are.
5. Q: Are Sara and Robert going to go to a museum?
   A: No, they're not. (They're going to see a movie.)
6. Q: Are Sara and Robert going to have dinner at a restaurant?
   A: No, they're not. (They're going to have dinner at Charlie's house.)

2 Wh-questions with *be going to*

A: What **are** you **going to do** this weekend?
B: I**'m going to have** a very busy weekend. My friend Ali **is going to visit** me, and we**'re going to spend** the weekend in the city.
A: That's nice. **Are** you **going to stay** in a hotel?
B: No, we**'re going to stay** with our friend Donna. And Donna **is going to have** a big party on Saturday night.
A: Really? And who**'s going to be** at the party? Do you know any of Donna's friends?
B: No, I don't. But Ali and I **are going to meet** everyone on Saturday night.

Unit 12

1 *Have* + noun; *feel* + adjective

A: **Hi, Chris. How are you?**
B: I'm terrific, thanks. How about you?
A: **I feel awful, actually.**
B: Oh, no! What's the matter?
A: **I think I have a fever.**
B: That's too bad. Do you have a headache?
A: **Yes, I do. And I have a stomachache, too.**
B: Are you going to see a doctor?
A: **Yes. I'm going to call my doctor in a few minutes.**
B: Well, feel better soon.
A: **Thanks.**

Unit 10

1 Simple present Wh-questions (page 65)

> ▶ Remember: *who = what person; where = what place; how often = what frequency; when = what days; what time = what time of day*
> ▶ Remember: use *do* or *does* after the question word.

Complete the questions with the correct question word and *do* or *does*. Then match the questions with the answers.

1. ..... What ..... sports ..... do ..... you like? ———— a. My father and my brother.
2. .... you go to games with? \ b. Usually at three o'clock.
3. .... often .... your team play? \ c. Baseball. I love to watch my team.
4. .... they play? d. Once a week.
5. .... they play? e. On Saturday afternoons.
6. .... time .... the games start? f. At Lincoln Park.

2 *Can* for ability (page 67)

> ▶ Use the base form of the verb with *can*. With third-person singular, don't add an *–s* to *can* or to the base form: She **can play** the piano. (NOT: ~~She can plays the piano.~~)

A Write sentences about the things people can and can't do. Use *can* or *can't* with *and, but,* or *or.* (✓ = can, ✗ = can't)

1. Sally: ride a bike ✓   drive a car ✗
   Sally can ride a bike, but she can't drive a car.
2. John: play the piano ✓   play the violin ✓
   ....
3. Brad and George: act ✓   sing ✗
   ....
4. Maria: snowboard ✓   ice-skate ✗
   ....
5. Justin: upload photos ✗   download a video ✗
   ....
6. Lisa: write poems ✗   tell good jokes ✓
   ....

B Look at part A. Answer the questions. Write short sentences.

1. Can Brad and George sing? *No, they can't.* ....
2. Who can tell good jokes? ....
3. Can Sally drive a car? ....
4. Can John play the piano? ....
5. Who can snowboard? ....
6. What can George do? ....

Unit 11

1 The future with *be going to* (page 73)

> ▶ Use *am/is/are* + *going to* + base form for the future: We**'re going to stay** home tonight.
>
> ▶ In questions with *be going to*, the *be* verb comes before the noun or pronoun: **Is he going to bake** me a cake?

A Complete Robert's story. Use the correct form of *be going to* and the verbs in parentheses.

Tomorrow ..*is going to be*.. (be) a very exciting day. It's my birthday, and my friends and I .... (celebrate). In the morning, Scott and I .... (drive) to the beach. Our friend Sara .... (meet) us there. We .... (stay) at the beach for a few hours. Then we .... (have) lunch at my favorite restaurant. After lunch, Scott .... (go) to work, and Sara and I .... (see) a movie. After the movie, we .... (go) to our friend Charlie's house. He .... (cook) dinner for Sara and me.

B Write questions. Then look at part A and answer the questions.

1. Robert / celebrate / with his family?
   Q: ..Is Robert going to celebrate with his family?..........
   A: ..No, he's going to celebrate with his friends...........
2. Scott and Robert / take the bus / to the beach?
   Q: ....
   A: ....
3. the friends / have lunch / at a restaurant?
   Q: ....
   A: ....
4. Sara and Robert / go to a museum?
   Q: ....
   A: ....
5. Sara and Robert / have dinner / at a restaurant?
   Q: ....
   A: ....

2 Wh-questions with *be going to* (page 75)

> ▶ Use *is* in questions with *Who* as the subject: **Who's** going to be there? (NOT: ~~Who are going to be there?~~)

Complete the conversation with the correct form of *be going to*.

A: What ....*are*.......... you ....*going to do*.... (do) this weekend?
B: I .... (have) a very busy weekend. My friend Ali .... (visit) me, and we .... (spend) the weekend in the city.
A: That's nice. .... you .... (stay) in a hotel?
B: No, we .... (stay) with our friend Donna. And Donna .... (have) a big party on Saturday night.
A: Really? And who .... (be) at the party? Do you know any of Donna's friends?
B: No, I don't. But Ali and I .... (meet) everyone on Saturday night.

Unit 12

1 *Have* + noun; *feel* + adjective (page 79)

▶ For most health problems, use *a/an*: I have **a** cold. I have **an** earache. With *flu*, use *the*: I have **the** flu. (NOT: ~~I have a flu.~~)

Complete the conversation. Use the sentences in the box.

> I think I have a fever.
> Thanks.
> I feel awful, actually.
> Yes. I'm going to call my doctor in a few minutes.
> Yes, I do. And I have a stomachache, too.
> ✓Hi, Chris. How are you?

A: Hi, Chris. How are you? ....

B: I'm terrific, thanks. How about you?

A: ....

B: Oh, no! What's the matter?

A: ....

B: That's too bad. Do you have a headache?

A: ....

B: Are you going to see a doctor?

A: ....

B: Well, feel better soon.

A: ....

2 Imperatives (page 82)

▶ Use the base form of the verb in affirmative imperatives: **Go** home and **rest**, Pat.
▶ Use *don't* + base form of the verb in negative imperatives. The form doesn't change: **Don't go** to school today, Pat.

Read the situations. Give the people advice. Use the phrases in the box.

> ✓drink coffee in the afternoon
> eat any cold food
> exercise today or tomorrow
> take an antacid
> take two aspirins
> work too hard

1. Dan can't sleep at night. Don't drink coffee in the afternoon. ....
2. Casey has a headache. ....
3. Kristina works 12 hours a day. ....
4. Michael has sore muscles. ....
5. Min-ho has a toothache. ....
6. Laila has an awful stomachache. ....

Grammar plus answer key

Unit 1

1 My, your, his, her

1. B: Hi, Carlos. What's **your** last name?
   A: It's Gonzales.
   B: How do you spell **your** last name? Is it G-O-N-Z-A-L-E-Z?
   A: No, it's G-O-N-Z-A-L-E-S. And what's **your** name?
   B: **My** name is Bill Powers. Nice to meet you.
2. A: What's Ms. Robinson's first name?
   B: **Her** first name is Katherine. **Her** nickname is Katie.
   A: I'm sorry. What's **her** first name again?
   B: It's Katherine. And what's Mr. Weber's first name?
   A: **His** first name is Peter.
   B: That's right. And his nickname is Pete.

2 The verb be

1. A: Excuse me. **Are** you Patty Wilson?
   B: No, **I'm not**. **She's** over there.
   A: OK. Thanks.
2. A: Hi. Are **you** Patty Wilson?
   C: Yes, **I am**.
   A: Oh, good. **I'm** Sergio Baez. **You're** in my English class.
   C: Yes, I **am**. **It's** nice to meet you, Sergio.

Unit 2

1 This/these; it/they; plurals

1. A: **What are** these?
   B: **They're** my **earrings**.
2. A: **What's** this?
   B: **It's a** cell phone.
3. A: What's **this**?
   B: **It's an** address book.

2 Yes/No and *where* questions with *be*

A

2. e   3. a   4. b   5. d

B

B: I don't know. Is **it** in your book bag?
A: No, **it's** not.
B: Is **this** your pen?
A: Yes, **it is**. Thanks! Now, **where** are my keys?
B: **Are they** on your desk?
A: Yes, **they are**. Thank you!

Unit 3

1 Negative statements and yes/no questions with *be*

A

2. We're not from London.
3. You and Tim are not in my class.
4. Spanish is not my first language./My first language is not Spanish.
5. My mother is not from Seoul.
6. They are not my keys.

B

1. B: No, **we're** not. **We're** from Guatemala.
2. A: **Is** your first language English?
   B: Yes, it **is**. My parents **are** from Australia.
3. A: **Are** Kenji and his friend Japanese?
   B: Yes, **they** are. But **they're / they are** in the U.S. now.
4. A: **Are** my mother and I late?
   B: No, **you're** not. **You're** early!

2 Wh-questions with *be*

2. **What** is her name? c
3. **What** is she like? f
4. **How** old is she? b
5. **Where** is your family from? a
6. **What** is Bangkok like? e

Unit 4

1 Possessives

1. A: **Whose** jacket is this? Is it **yours**, Phil?
   B: No, it's not **mine**. Ask Nick. I think it's **his**.
2. A: These aren't **our** books. Are they **yours**?
   B: No, they're not **ours**. Maybe they're Young-min's.
3. A: **Whose** sweaters are these? Are they Julie's?
   B: No, they're not **her** sweaters. But these shorts are **hers**.

2 Present continuous statements; conjunctions

2. It's raining.
3. I'm not wearing sunglasses.
4. You're not / You aren't wearing a new suit.
5. Michiko is wearing gloves.